B

A Sociological Approach to

Social Problems

THE STUDENTS LIBRARY OF SOCIOLOGY

GENERAL EDITOR: ROY EMERSON
Professor of Sociology
University of East Anglia

A Sociological Approach to Social Problems

by Noel Timms

*Lecturer in the Department of Social Science
London School of Economics*

LONDON

ROUTLEDGE AND KEGAN PAUL
NEW YORK: THE HUMANITIES PRESS

First published 1967
by Routledge and Kegan Paul Ltd
Broadway House, 68-74 Carter Lane
London, E.C.4

Printed in Great Britain
by Bookprint Limited
Crawley, Sussex

General editor's introduction

Today Sociology is going through a phase of great expansion. Not only is there a widespread general interest in the subject, but there is a rapid growth in the number of new courses at Universities, Training Colleges, and elsewhere. As a result there is an increasing number of potential readers of introductory textbooks. Some will be motivated by general interest; some will want to find out enough about the subject to see whether they would like to pursue a formal course in it; and others will already be following courses into which an element of Sociology has been fused. One approach to these readers is by means of the comprehensive introductory volume giving a general coverage of the field of sociology; another is by means of a series of monographs each providing an introduction to a selected topic. Both these approaches have their advantages and disadvantages. *The Students Library of Sociology* adopts the second approach. It will cover a more extensive range of topics than could be dealt with in a single volume; while at the same time each volume will provide a thorough introductory treatment of any one topic. The reader who has little or no knowledge in the field will find within any particular book a foundation upon which to build, and to extend by means of the suggestions for further reading.

In this volume Mr. Timms explores a field which is much more complex than might appear from its title. Firstly, it is necessary to consider what constitutes a social problem. If asked to make a list of social problems no doubt most people would include crime, and possibly poverty and no doubt some would include racism, but probably not many would include war. Yet it could be argued that the implications of the last are of at least

GENERAL EDITOR'S INTRODUCTION

equal importance for society to those of the previous ones. Is there any way of defining a social problem which will be theoretically meaningful? In other words, must we simply accept as social problems those areas of social behaviour which as a matter of fact have been treated as such or can we find some means of understanding certain types of social behaviour in terms of our understanding of the way social systems work?

This leads directly in to another set of considerations. For if some means can be found of understanding social problems in the sense I have suggested, this would constitute a sociological approach to their study. The topics covered in this book are directly related to much of the misunderstanding of what sociology is about. It is usual nowadays to label as sociological any discussion concerned, however loosely, with 'Society'. But a careful reading of Mr. Timms' treatment of the problem areas he has chosen should make clear the difference between this use of the adjective in everyday speech, and its more vigorous technical usage.

In dealing with his subject Mr. Timms makes use of the concepts of sociology such as 'role', 'norms', 'social control', 'class', and 'family'. These concepts are dealt with in other volumes in the series and reference should be made to them.

A. R. EMERSON

Contents

General editor's introduction   page v

1   Sociology and social problems   1

   A sociological approach   2
   Social relations   3
   Social facts   7
   Social structure   7
   Social problems   10
   Kinds of social problem   12
   Deviant behaviour and social disorganisation   14
   Conclusion   16

2   Sociological approaches to social problems   18

   Conflict and consensus   18
   The process of deviation   21
   The structural approach   24
   Summary   31

3   Sociology and crime   33

   The size and shape of the problem   33
   Sociological factors   37
   The ecological view   39
   The idea of a delinquent sub-culture   41
   Lower-class life itself as the milieu for gang
     delinquency   44
   Delinquency as the expression of subterranean
     values   46
   Delinquency as the solution of a problem   48

4   Sociology and mental illness   51

   The size and shape of the problem   51
   Social class factors   56
   The contribution of the sociologist   58
   The study of therapeutic organisations   59

CONTENTS

Sociological study of the 'causes' of mental illness   *page* 65

The sociological characterisation of mental illness   69

A critique of mental health concepts   71

5   The family and social problems   74

The family as the 'basic' unit   74
A way of looking at the family   78
Individual needs   80
Social norms   82
Social goals   85
Family identity   86

6   Summary and suggestions for further reading   90

Guide to further reading   96

Bibliography   101

I

Sociology and social problems

Definitions have their place, and this is, more often than not, at the conclusion rather than the beginning of a study. Yet the attempt to make a sociological approach to social problems involves us at the outset in problems of definition of two distinct kinds. An approach that is decisively sociological needs to be identified among the increasing number of viewpoints that are described by that name, and to be distinguished from the contributions that can be expected from the neighbouring discipline of psychology and the field of study known as social administration. We also need to consider the part played by the process of *social* definition in the delineation of certain aspects of social life as problems. In other words, we are raising in terms of definition two important kinds of question: Are 'social problems' simply ways of referring to aggregates of deviant individuals? Are these problems purely those 'evils' that a society at a particular time defines as a social problem by taking a variety of measures to cure or prevent it?

A sociological approach

The adjective 'social' is now used in connection with such a very wide variety of subjects that it is nearly drained of meaning. The same could almost be said of sociology. On television, for example, any investigation, however slight, into people's habits, any report of their spontaneous replies to scarcely formulated questions is classed as 'sociological'. Durkheim's words in regard to the misuse of the term 'social' are as relevant today as they were at the end of the last century: he observed that it 'is currently employed for practically all phenomena generally diffused within a society, however small their social interest. But on this basis there are, as it were, no human events that may not be called social' (Durkheim, 1894). The attempt to remedy this situation, and to anchor the 'social' and the 'sociological' more securely faces the fact that sociologists themselves are divided on a number of key issues. Is the sociologist primarily concerned with the investigation of social problems with a view to finding solutions, or with the investigation of problems relevant to the testing of hypotheses deduced from gradually developing theories about society? Does the sociologist aim at investigating society as the natural scientist studies non-human phenomena, or should he hope to *understand* the views and ideas of those who participate in any particular social system? Is sociology a profession or a discipline? As a professional the sociologist would be seen as someone trained in the methods which alone equip people to study 'sociological' problems, but if sociology is seen as a discipline then reference is to the study of society by any appropriate method, and the methods are open to anyone provided they can use them effectively.

These are large questions which will be more fully

discussed in other works in this series. What concerns us here is not the delineation of the features of sociology with a loving and time-consuming attention to the precise form and place of each distinguishing mark, in order to distinguish rigidly between, for instance, history and sociology. Rather our concern is with those features of sociology that might justifiably claim to constitute a distinctive approach to the study of social problems. The case can rest on such specifically sociological concepts as those of the social relation and social structure. It is these concepts that most readily establish the contribution of sociology to the understanding of social problems compared with that of psychology and social administration. These disciplines play an important part in the study of social problems, but there has been a tendency, particularly in the case of psychology, to assume that social problems can be most easily understood in terms of the actions of maladjusted individuals. The influence of psychological maladjustment is considerable, but we cannot simply assume that psychological factors are always primary. Ideally, we should perhaps hope for a combined sociological and psychological understanding of social problems, but this assumes that we are relatively clear about the distinctive nature of each approach.

Social relations

The most fruitful discussion of social relations is to be found in Weber (1962). He begins with a consideration of social conduct. This is seen essentially as conduct orientated towards the conduct of others, whether this is in the past, the present or the future. The others to whom we are orientated may be known or unknown or they may constitute an indefinite quantity. As an example of this last possibility Weber cites the exchange of money.

In this activity an individual's conduct is based on the expectation that in the unspecified future numerous but unknown and undertermined 'others' will accept money as a means of exchange. The definition of social conduct offered is very wide, but not every kind of conduct can properly be described as social; there are limits. Conduct is non-social if it is orientated exclusively to the behaviour of inanimate objects; subjective attitudes are to be considered as social behaviour only if they are orientated to the behaviour of others. The social character is not bestowed on every type of contact between human beings, but only where the individual's conduct is meaningfully related to that of others.

On the basis of this idea of social conduct Weber proceeds to characterise the social relation or social relationship. He states that 'the term "social relationship" will be used to designate the situation where two or more persons are engaged in conduct wherein each takes account of the behaviour of the other in a meaningful way and is therefore orientated in these terms. The social relationship thus *consists* of the *probability* that individuals will behave in some meaningfully determinable way' (p. 63). This is a general characterisation of the social relationship, but the content of any particular relationship will, of course, vary. 'Its content may be most varied: conflict, hostility, sexual attraction, friendship, loyalty or market exchange; it may involve the "fulfilment" or "evasion" or "severance" of an agreement; economic, erotic, or any other form of "competition"; a sharing of occupations or membership in the same class or nation' (p. 63).

The idea of the expectation of social action is in itself significant, but two important points need to be kept in mind. The first is that the social relation is not itself directly observable. The phenomena that are observable, and from which the existence of a social relation may be

4

deduced, have been listed as follows by Rex (1961, p. 53):

(1) the actor's purpose or interest,
(2) his expectations of 'the other's' behaviour,
(3) the other's purposes and the actor's knowledge of them,
(4) the norms which the actor knows the other accepts,
(5) the other's desire to win and keep the actor's approval.

Secondly, it must not be assumed that in every or even in most cases there will be complete and harmonious reciprocity between the actor and the other. Weber himself stated—and more weight should have been given to this—'A social relationship in which the attitudes are completely and fully oriented toward each other is really a marginal case' (Weber, p. 65).

The concept of the social relationship directs our attention to important areas in the study of social problems. It helps us to see that society is not somehow a total phenomenon set over and against 'the individual', and that the individual is in dynamic interaction with other social beings and not simply responding to overwhelming pressure or moulding some inert environmental mass. The concept also helps us to distinguish a specifically sociological contribution from that of the student of social administration. If we take the question of money, already mentioned, we shall find that whereas the psychologist may be interested in its symbolic significance, or the development of attitudes towards money in particular groups (e.g. children), the student of social administration is characteristically concerned with the distribution of income. This concern arises primarily from an interest in the incomes, assumed inadequate, of the 'underprivileged'. Data on the national income is collected not so much in order to understand the social system—for example, how money comes to be associated with privilege and how privilege shows itself in a particular society—but in order to demonstrate unfairness and to show how those who are unfairly treated might be compensated. If income was ever equitably redistributed the interest of the student of social administration would shift. If he were to persist in his study on the grounds that such a redistribution would be impermanent, this would demonstrate clearly that he was working on certain assumptions about his society, which would require closer investigation. It is these assumptions that are the sociologist's centre of interest. For the sociologist data on the distribution of income is but a starting point for exploring the positions in the system of the social relations of production of individuals with incomes of varying size.

This kind of difference between sociology and social administration can be illustrated from a fairly recent study of so-called 'problem families' (Wilson, 1962). This work describes very well the economic pressures on the 'problem family', and advocates certain changes in such matters as the policy of the National Assistance Board. Yet the factors influencing the families are judged primarily from a humanitarian viewpoint which, valid though it may be, has no necessary place in sociology. Sociology today often appears to provide a moral criticism of society in terms which seem to be more or less acceptable to the age, but when it is most moral it is in danger of being least sociological, since it is often using unexamined assumptions about the society in which it is situated. In this study of the problem family data on family budgets, on income and on such facts as the handicap of one or both marriage partners are important from the viewpoint of administrative action, but the pattern of social relations in this data is left uninvestigated.

Social facts

Yet, when due allowance is made for the importance of social relationships and for their complexity, must it not be admitted that such relationships occur between individuals, and that in the last analysis societies are nothing but groups of individuals? If this is the case, should we not look to psychology for our basic under-standing of people and, therefore, of their problems? Some sociologists have based their denial of this position on the existence of 'social facts' that exist independently of any individuals influenced by them. Durkheim, for example, argued strongly for social facts as a distinct class of facts that constituted the social determinants of behaviour, and were external from the point of view of the actor. He spoke, for example, of 'currents of opinion' as social facts. 'Currents of opinion, with an intensity varying according to the time and place, *impel* certain groups either to more marriages, for example, or to more suicides, or to a higher or lower birth rate etc. These currents are plainly social facts. At first sight they seem inseparable from the forms they take in individual cases. But statistics furnish us with a means of isolating them' (italics not original) (Durkheim, 1894). The concept of 'social facts' is a way of referring to the sociological determinants of behaviour, but the search for such facts existing independently of all individuals in a society can hardly hope to be fruitful. As Rex (1961) has suggested, the social determinants of behaviour are external from the point of view of the actor whose actions are being explained, but they are not external to *all* individuals.

Social structure

Perhaps a more fruitful way of expressing the idea of

sociological determinants is to think not so much of the
individual (the individual is after all a highly complex
and abstract concept), but of the various positions that
he comes to occupy in any society, and of the different
and often competing groups of which he is a member.
The positions or roles that a person occupies are to be
found in any society in significant clusters which we call
institutions. These social institutions and the most
important groups in a society constitute a society's social
structure, which, to use a phrase of the Webbs (1932,
p. 17), 'can be known and described as such, irrespective
of the human beings whom it concerns, though not without them'. It is this idea of social structure that often
distinguishes the work of the sociologist from that of the
psychologist or social psychologist. For instance, Klein
(1965, Vol. II, p. 631) sums up the position in society
of the deprived or submerged group as follows: 'The
characteristic culture patterns of other levels of the society
will not have had any great direct effect on the individuals
of this sub-culture, though of course their *unfortunate*
position is maintained by the general social and economic
arrangements of the total society' (italics not original).
In fact the position of these individuals *as* deprived or
submerged can only be understood in relation to some
notion of the structure of their society. Relationships are
moreover likely to exist on a two-way basis between a
submerged section or group and other groups and social
institutions. A similar kind of criticism has been raised
in connection with the important psychological study,
'The Authoritarian Personality' (Hyman and Skeatsley,
1954). The argument of this work was that a person's
political, economic and social convictions form a coherent
pattern which is the expression of deep-seated personality
traits. In particular, the personality structure which gives
rise to anti-minority sentiments is derived from actual

early family experiences. These sentiments, it is argued, could not be derived solely from such external factors as social status, group membership or religion. It has been suggested, with some plausibility, that the sample on which the study was based enabled the investigators to discount the social, cultural and personality differences associated with social class differences, and that the complexity of social structure was reduced in the study to a question of membership of a few groups.

Criticisms of this kind, however, should not be taken to imply that a sociological is somehow *better* than a psychological approach. Each has a distinctive contribution to make. Yet the social determinants of behaviour must always be recognised. Even Freud noted the influence of social class factors, though he did not develop much curiosity about them. He described (Freud, 1935, p. 308-9) what he considered to be the differential results of mutual sex play on two children, one the child of the caretaker and the other of the owner of the house. 'The final result,' wrote Freud, 'will be very different in the two children. The caretaker's daughter will continue masturbation, perhaps up to the onset of menstruation, and then give it up without difficulty . . . she will be unharmed by the premature sexual activity, free from neurosis, and able to live her life. Very different is the result in the other child. She will very soon, while yet a child, acquire sense of having done wrong; after a fairly short time, she will give up the masturbatory satisfaction, though perhaps only with a tremendous struggle, but will nevertheless retain an inner feeling of subdued depression. . . . When the time comes for a man to choose her as a wife, the neurosis will break out and cheat her out of marriage and the joy of life.' The story suggests the importance of class differences in child rearing, but it should not be supposed that the ways of bringing children up can be easily changed or manipulated. Argyle, for example, in a recent study (1964, p. 117) suggests that 'If society encouraged some kinds of child-rearing technique and discouraged others, it would be possible to have fewer delinquents and mental patients and a greater number of happy, effective and creative individuals.' This, however, neglects the complex connections between child-rearing techniques and the structure of any society, and underrates the extent to which society becomes, as it were, a component of personality not just in the individual's so-called formative years, but throughout his life. The way in which society plays its part in the inner life of the individual can be seen in the following brief extract from Virginia Woolf (*A Writer's Diary*, p. 324-25). 'I'm loosely anchored. Further, the war—our waiting while the knives sharpen—has taken away the outer wall of security. No echo comes back. I have no summer drugs. . . . Those familiar circumlocutions—those standards—which have for so many years given back an echo and so thickened my identity are all wide and wild as the desert now.'

Social problems

If each reader of this book made a short list of the most serious contemporary social problems and then compared it with the lists of, say, half a dozen others, he would probably discover important differences in priority. Some would place delinquency, for example, above mental illness, and vice versa. He would also begin to see perhaps that people saw social problems differently. It would not occur to some people to define road accidents or marital disharmony as social problems. Finally, the reader might find in himself and in others a tendency to regard one particular problem as *the* social problem. This tendency is certainly apparent in any historical survey of those who have written about social problems (the social pathologists). Hobson, for instance (1902), considered that waste of work and life were the source of all social problems. Until the 1930's and beyond there is a very evident tendency to regard mental subnormality as the source of a considerable range of social problems. The Wood Committee on Mental Deficiency, for example, stated that if we could segregate all families containing a mental defective of the primary amentia type (i.e. where no developmental or environmental 'cause' can be found) we would discover we had collected a significant social group. 'It would include . . . a much larger proportion of insane persons, epileptics, paupers, criminals (especially recidivists), unemployables, habitual slum dwellers, prostitutes, inebriates and other social inefficients than would a group of families not containing mental defectives' (1929). It is perhaps not surprising that in view of this chronicle of distressing, if very disparate, conditions the Committee decided to call this section of the community the 'social problem group'.

The inclination to assume that one condition or problem is at the root of all others is in itself a fact of some interest. From the point of view of the study of social problems, however, it is preferable to take the more pessimistic approach outlined by Christopher Fry:

One always thinks if only
One particular unpleasantness
Could be cleared up, life would become as promising
As always it was promising to be.
But in fact we merely change anxieties.
                    (*The Dark is Light Enough.* Act III)

Yet the way any society defines a 'particular unpleasantness' and changes one anxiety for another is of considerable importance.

Generally speaking, a social problem can be seen as 'a significant discrepancy between social standards and social actuality' (Merton and Nisbet, 1961, p. 701). At least two terms in this definition require discussion : 'significant', and 'social standards'.

Kinds of social problem

To which groups will the discrepancy be significant, and can we speak of degrees of significance from the point of view of society as a whole? It has been suggested that there are different kinds of social problem to be distinguished in terms of the different groups involved in the social process of defining the phenomena as a social problem. Five kinds of problem have been suggested (St. Clair Drake, 1955): (a) problems which involve popular concern arising from mass experience, for example, unemployment in Great Britain in the 1930's; (b) problems involving large-scale concern stimulated by the mass media of communication, of which juvenile delinquency is perhaps a good example; (c) problems which involve economic interest groups threatened by the wider society; here we might consider motoring organisations seeking to define the problem of road casualties in terms of bad roads as opposed to bad driving; (d) problems which involve the interests of small humanitarian groups, like the N.S.P.C.C.; and, finally, (e) problems which involve the activities of *élite* groups and administrators who from strategic positions in the social structure have access to relevant information, and on the basis of this knowledge are able to conceptualise a social problem. A good example of this kind of activity is to be found in the nineteenth century in the work of Edwin Chadwick and a small group of administrators whose actions led to the creation of what has been termed 'the Mid-Victorian Administrative State' to deal with a range of newly appreciated social problems.

This attempted characterisation of social problems at least has the advantage of calling our attention to the important part played by interest groups (large or small) in defining a discrepancy between standards and actuality as sufficiently significant to constitute a social problem. Why should such groups have an interest in so defining a social condition? A consideration of the term 'social problem' may help us to begin to see some answers to this question. If we define a condition as a *social* problem we argue that its source is to be found in social relations, in society, and that its remedy is to be sought in some kind of social action. A stress on the second part of the term, social *problem*, involves us psychologically, if not logically, in a world in which 'problem' goes with 'solution'. It is not really worth defining a condition as a problem if the only possible response is that of endurance. However, it is very likely that a workable and effective solution of a 'social problem' will not be found at the outset, and it is important to note that the social definition of social problems changes. Delinquency was at different times defined as a problem of sub-normality of intelligence, of a reaction to an impoverished environment, of emotional disturbance and so on. Indeed, there is a significant activity amongst social problem definers which consists in social problem re-definition. For instance, the social problem of the young mother who goes out to work is not 'really' that she is neglectful, but that other groups in society have failed to make adequate provision for what might be considered an imperative social need, that she should work.

Deviant behaviour and social disorganisation

So far, we have discussed 'significance' from the point of view of the participants. Should the term be used in this restricted sense? Should we not consider as social problems those conditions of social malfunctioning that are revealed by a sociological analysis even though the members of the society remain ignorant of them as problems? This ignorance could take one of two forms. Members of a society or a group might define some behaviour as problematic, but a sociological study might reveal that though a problem existed they had described it wrongly. Weiss and Riessman (in Merton and Nisbet, 1961) warn us to be sceptical where we find wide agreement that something constitutes 'a problem': 'For any really exigent problem is partly a product of a more general malaise; that is, in some way it represents a solution to still other problems.' They give as an example the definition as a problem of the operation by factory workers of informal limits on production. They suggest that this problem is a solution to the problem created by the inability of management to call the workers to help to set goals for production: quota restriction is one possible solution to what might otherwise be continuous conflict.

The second kind of ignorance of the nature of the social problems contained in any particular society is more complex: it is a question not of faulty or inadequate description but of ignorance about failure in the social system. Merton, in a useful discussion of social problems (Merton and Nisbet, 1961, p. 720), has distinguished deviant behaviour from social disorganisation. Deviant behaviour is behaviour departing significantly from the norm, but social disorganisation refers to 'inadequacies or failures in a social system of interrelated

14

statuses and roles such that the collective purposes and individual objectives of its members are less fully realized than they could be in an alternative workable system.' These inadequacies are seen as failures to meet one or more of the functional requirements of the system: (a) social patterns of behaviour are not maintained; (b) personal tensions generated within the system are insufficiently controlled, canalised and siphoned off; (c) the social system is inadequately related to its environment, neither controlling it nor adapted to it; (d) the structure of the system does not allow sufficient scope for members to attain the goals which are its *raison d'être*; (e) relations between members do not maintain the minimum cohesion necessary to carry out valued activities. It is in the realm of these and other functional failures that participants are most likely to be unaware of the existence of social problems. The sociologist can, however, as Merton indicates, contribute to the analysis of such failures. It would be maintaining an unreal limitation to suggest that the sociologist must only concern himself with the problems that particular groups in a society define as 'social problems'. There are problems of varying importance in any social structure. Thus, our conception of significance (in 'a significant discrepancy between social standards and social actuality') must be correspondingly enlarged.

It remains to consider the second term in the definition 'social standards'. This will be discussed more fully in Chapter 5. At this stage it is important to see that questions of value are inseparable from a study of social problems. Obviously, judgments of value are made when a condition is defined as a problem: some action ought to be taken. Of greater significance is the part played by values in the creation of social problems. Lemert (1951, p. 412), for example, commenting on the Mental Hygiene Movement, has suggested that 'The suspicion is a strong one that this movement is a contemporary manifestation of values in our culture which, if not part of the process producing mental disorders, at least conspire to defeat efforts at scientific understanding and complete rehabilitation of mentally deranged persons.' At the heart of most if not all social problems is a conflict of interests and of values. Finally, value judgments prevent members of a society from agreeing on solutions to social problems. This failure of agreement stems from the fact that people will not abandon those values which are a formal cause of the condition that is regarded as undesirable. This position can easily become exaggerated. Thus, Fuller (1939) has suggested that 'our sacred worship of monogamous marriage *compels* the unwed mother to neglect her child' (italics not original). Nonetheless, differences of value surrounding marriage and the family make it difficult for people to agree on the solution of the problem of the unmarried mother.

Conclusion

A sociological approach does not consist in the collection of facts about discrete aspects of the environment, even though, as we shall see, statistical investigation may well be a necessary preliminary for sociological study. It is rather the attempt to discover those social relations that 'make sense' of facts about income, occupational status and so on. Nor is a sociological approach confined exclusively to external factors. It is concerned also with those aspects of social relations which become part of the individual's inner world. Durkheim's (1947, p. 61) picture of the social relationship convinces us of this: 'The image of the one who completes us becomes inseparable from ours, not only because it is frequently associated with ours, but particularly because it is the natural

complement of it. It thus becomes an integral and perma-
nent part of our conscience, to such a point that we can
no longer separate ourselves from it and seek to increase
its force.'

In making a sociological approach to social problems
we are not necessarily concerned with finding solutions
acceptable to participants. Nor are we concerned with
such important questions as why people become the kind
of people who are criminal, mentally ill and so on. Rather
we try to understand the processes of the social definition
of social problems, and also the structural problems of
a society of which the participants may not be aware.

We try to delineate those features of social relations
and of the social structure which determine the kind and
the distribution of deviant acts, and also more importantly,
of deviant careers. In discovering and describing the
problems of any particular society we shall probably
learn what is one of the most valuable lessons of the
sociological approach, namely that social problems do not
necessarily arise from conditions judged to be pathological;
they are often the side-effects of valued ideas and
activities.

2

Sociological approaches to social problems

Conflict and consensus

So far we have seen the importance of the processes whereby particular aspects of social behaviour are defined as 'social problems', and of viewing both those who define and the problems to which they attend as parts of a wider configuration. In defining social problems generally as 'a significant discrepancy between social standards and social actuality' we have discussed the ideas of 'significance' and of 'social standards': we should now examine the notion of 'discrepancy'. What have sociologists to say about its nature?

The American literature on social problems is extensive. Some writers attempt to present a rounded theoretical approach to social problems generally, whilst others offer a less unified approach in which statistics on incidence and prevalence jostle with ideas on the varying cultural levels of different groups (e.g. native-born compared to immigrants), the place of the small group in social control and so on. In Britain there has been little if any general theorising about social problems. Consequently, it is to the American literature that we must turn in order to begin to find examples of a sociological approach to the study of social problems in general. Before, however, we select for consideration some of these approaches, it is important to grasp at least some of the implications of the fact that in sociology today can be found two contrasting models of society. Dahrendorf (1959) has termed these two views of the social world, the integration theory and the coercion theory.

These theories can be stated in an extreme form, so that any one writer's views could be said to approximate to one or other of the positions. According to the integration theory, every society is a relatively persistent, stable structure of elements. These elements are well integrated with each other, and every element has a function, i.e. it contributes to the maintenance of society as a system. Every functioning social structure is based on a consensus of values among its members. In contrast to these ideas the coercion theory states that every society is at every point subject to processes of change; social change is ubiquitous. Every society displays at every point dissensus and conflict, and every element in society contributes to the disintegration of the system. Each social structure is based, not on a consensus of values, but on the coercion of some by others. Dahrendorf argues that both these theories are necessary for an understanding of society. It would appear, however, that in the study of social problems it is the integration theory that has predominated.

This relative predominance of the integration theory as opposed to the conflict theory can be seen in a characterisation by Mills (1943) of the typical social pathologist. His essay is based on a study of a large number of American social pathologists, which could with profit be repeated on comparable British material.

Amongst the pathologists Mills notes certain 'persuasive ways of defining social problems'. Firstly, problems are often described in terms of deviation from the norms, but the norms themselves are rarely investigated. Few if any attempts have been made to explain deviations from the norms in terms of the quality of the norms themselves, and explanations usually refer to biological impulses which 'break through' or to inadequate socialisation which is seldom defined. Secondly, problems are often seen as arising from 'situations', but these are not connected to any structure. The social pathologists, according to Mills, speak in terms of 'society' and 'the social order', but such terms suffer from a formal emptiness and, often also, from moralistic undertones. In fact, 'society' is seen largely in terms of small communities and primary groups. 'Pathological' behaviour is not viewed as in some way 'incompatible' with an existing structure, but as behaviour which is contrary to certain humanitarian ideals. Mills suggests that it is an imagined small rural community that is often the assumed model against which pathology is judged, and there has certainly been a strong element of what could be termed 'the arcadian mystique' in many proposals for social reform in this country, from Barnett's country holidays in the nineteenth century to the Garden City in the twentieth.

In considering, then, sociological descriptions and explanations of social problems, we should remain alert to the possibility that the terms in which these descriptions and explanations are couched can be seen as themselves the expression of a social ideology. We have also to remember that social problems are seen as manifestations of social malfunctioning that are very variously described in the literature. Each different description has implications that should be carefully traced. Thus, the conditions giving rise to social problems have been described as states of social pathology (Gillin, 1946; Wootton, 1959; Lemert, 1951), of social disorganisation (Elliott and Merrill, 1961), and of dissensus and deviation (Dynes *et al.*, 1964). These varying descriptions cannot be seen as so many different attempts to talk about the same series of objects. Disorganisation, for instance, implies a break-down in the *orderly* processes of social interaction, whilst social pathology implies a sickness in the body politic which is, presumably, normally in a state of health. One way of classifying the various sociological approaches would be to use these and other general descriptions.

For our present purposes, however, differences between sociological approaches can be illustrated by examining in some detail an example of the approach that lays stress on the process of becoming deviant, and an example that emphasises a structural approach.

The process of deviation

Lemert (1951) distinguishes between individual deviation, as in the case of the exceptional child, or musical genius, and situational deviation. He recognises that 'situation' is a sociological term that has been widely used to refer to social institutions, to social relationships or to almost any aspect of an existing environment. He reserves the term to cover pressures arising from persons and groups external to the individual which are relatively more force-ful than internal pressures. Some situational deviation takes the form of random and unstable deviant reactions, but other situational deviation is cumulative. In cumu-lative situational deviation a large segment of the popu-lation is involved, and the deviation is facilitated by the knowledge that other people in the society have met situations of conflict, in atypical or socially disapproved ways. The conflict that Lemert sees in both types of situational deviation is primarily a culture conflict.

In examining the process whereby a person actually becomes deviant Lemert makes a useful distinction between primary and secondary deviation. Primary deviation is situational and occasional, and remains so as long as it can be dealt with as part of a socially accept-able role. This can be achieved, for instance, by means of the techniques of neutralisation, to be discussed in Chapter 3. In these circumstances, suggests Lemert, be-haviour that is in accordance with the norm and behav-iour that is contrary remain strange and 'somewhat tensional bedfellows' in the same person. Secondary deviation follows on this primary stage when a person reacts to his own primary deviant behaviour which in its turn has been subject to social reaction. As the be-haviour which is deviant is sustained it becomes dis-ruptive to those in social interaction with the deviant. Meanwhile, the individual who has been expressing primary deviation begins perhaps to react symbolically to his own changed behaviour, his deviant acts. He begins to include this deviant behaviour as part of his self-definition, and to organise it into active roles. He begins to use these roles as a means of defence, attack or adjust-ment to the problems created by the consequent societal reaction to him. As Lemert says, at each step in the passage from primary to secondary deviation there is an increasing mutual reinforcement of a deviant self-conception and the social response to it. When societal definitions and their subjective counterpart apply over an increasing range of the person's behaviour, the choice of role is narrowed to one kind of role, namely deviance. Yet there is, of course, no general role of deviant, people deviate in particular ways. So why do people follow particular secondary deviationary careers? Some sociolo-gists would argue that there is no demonstrable stability in the choice of sociopathic roles. Lemert, however, argues that we cannot assume there are *no* limits on the choice of these roles. He lists a number of limitations, external and internal. Amongst the former he refers to age, sex and physical characteristics which produce social barriers which may exclude the deviant from many general social roles and from participation in some sociopathic groups. Internal limitations consist of such limits as those imposed by lack of knowledge and of skill.

These views of Lemert can be taken as a good example of a sociological approach that emphasises the processes whereby deviant acts come to be committed and deviant careers to be made. What contribution do they make to an understanding of the *discrepancy* between social standards and social actuality that constitutes a social problem?

The theory of 'process' perhaps makes two main contributions. Firstly, it emphasises the important part played by social reaction to deviant acts, which interacts with a gradually changing conception of the self. Deviance, according to this approach, is the result of a slow, complex process. As Lemert has argued in a later publication (Clinard, 1964) a sociological theory of deviance must focus specifically upon the social inter-actions which not only define the behaviour as deviant, but also organise and activate the application of sanctions by individuals, groups and agencies. Social control in this context must be seen as an independent variable rather than as either an assumed constant quantity or a simple kind of social reflex action to deviance. This constitutes an important sociological contribution to the study of social problems.

Secondly, the approach encourages us to examine more closely both deviance and conformity, which are both seen as problematic. For Lemert the individual is not a relatively free agent 'choosing' adaptations to a consistent and stable order of values. He is rather a person who is, to varying degrees, 'captured' by the claims of the various groups to which he has given his allegiance. His overt behaviour, whether it is conforming or deviant, frequently reflects a compromise. Persons caught up in a network of conflicting claims and values do not choose deviant solutions as such, but they sometimes choose courses of action which carry risks of deviation.

The structural approach

The structural approach to the explanation of social problems that has been most developed is that contained in Merton's (1957) application of the idea of *anomie*. As Cohen has stated, 'Without any doubt, this body of ideas, which has come to be known as "anomie theory", has been the most influential single formulation in the sociology of deviance in the last twenty-five years' (quoted, Clinard, p. 10). The idea of 'anomie' was first propounded by Durkheim, who used it in discussing the problem of explaining social solidarity in an increasingly differentiated society. In the new industrial society Durkheim saw anomie (or normlessness) as the main abnormal condition. It arose because the division of labour failed to produce sufficiently effective contacts between members of the society and an adequate regulation of relationships. Later, in his study of suicide, Durkheim used the idea of anomie to classify one of the different types of suicide that he identified. Anomic suicide was a product of a situation in which there were no effective social restraints on aspirations that had become boundless. In a situation of anomie, 'The limits are unknown between the possible and the impossible, what is just and what is unjust, legitimate claims and hopes and those which are immoderate. Consequently, there is no restraint upon aspirations. If the disturbance is profound, it affects even the principles controlling the distribution of men among various occupations' (Durkheim, 1952, p. 253). This situation of anomie is contrasted with more normal social conditions when 'a genuine regimen exists [which] . . . fixes with relative precision the maximum degree of ease of living to which each social class may legitimately aspire'. The average level of need for each social condition should, according to Durkheim, be regulated, and another, more precise rule should fix the way in which these conditions are open to individuals. The society that is in a state of anomie is perhaps rather like the unmarried man, who, says Durkheim (p. 271), 'aspires to everything and is satisfied with nothing.'

Merton has used the concept of anomie within the general argument that social structures exert a definite pressure on certain persons (or persons in certain social positions) to engage in non-conforming behaviour of various kinds. To advance this argument he makes an important distinction between the ends and means in any society. On the one hand, there are culturally defined goals, purposes and interests 'held out as legitimate objectives for all or for diversely located members of the society' (1957, p. 132). These goals are more or less integrated with each other and ordered in some hierarchy of values. On the other hand, there are culturally-standardised practices which define, regulate and control the acceptable means of reaching or trying to reach the prescribed goals. Using this distinction Merton can identify both conformity, when both the goals and the means are accepted, and also various kinds of anomic response. The following table shows what these are and how they are related to acceptance $(+)$ or rejection of $(-)$ cultural goals or the means of striving for their attainment.

	Modes of Individual Adaptation	Cultural Goals	Institutional Means
1.	Conformity	+	+
2.	Innovation	+	−
3.	Ritualism	−	+
4.	Retreatism	−	−

The disjunction with which Merton is preoccupied is that which he considers prevails in the United States, namely the emphasis on the cultural goal of success and the fact that many people in the society are deprived of access to the institutionalised means of reaching for these goals which are held to be legitimate and possible for all members of the society; 'when poverty and associated disadvantages in competing for the culture values approved for *all* members of the society are linked with a cultural emphasis on pecuniary success as a dominant goal, high rates of criminal behaviour are the normal outcome' (Merton, 1957, p. 147). In a later consideration of his approach Merton (1964) argued that the emphasis on success in an open class society was more widespread than in a society dominated by ascribed status, and that appreciable numbers of people became estranged from a society that promised them in principle what they were denied in reality.

Before considering some of the main extensions and criticisms of the anomic approach two features should be stressed. In the first place this is not a theory about psychological states. The categories above 'refer to role behaviour in specific types of situations, not to personality. They are types of more or less enduring response, not types of personality organisation' (Merton, 1957, p. 140). In an attempt (not altogether successful) to preserve the distinction between the description of a property of the social structure and of a state of mind it has become customary to refer to the latter in terms of anomia. The distinction clearly is important, and mention should be made in this context of Srole's (1956) work on the construction of a scale of anomia. Srole has suggested that anomia can be measured by the extent to which an individual (a) senses that the leaders of his community are detached from, and indifferent to, his needs, (b) perceives that he and others like him are actually retrogressing from goals they had already reached, (d) sees life as meaningless because of the loss of norms and values, (e) finds that the framework of his immediate personal relationships provides neither support nor a sufficiently firm basis on which he can predict his future. Yet, important as the distinction between anomia and anomie is, it is still easy to slip from talking about the property of a social structure to discussing elements of people's states of mind (which *may* be connected with conditions in the social structure). Even Merton (1964) has suggested that 'There is a *streak* of the innovator, of the ritualist, retreatist, and rebel in most of us' (italics not original).

Secondly, Merton's approach does not assume that the cultural goal of monetary success is actually internalised in all strata in society. He refers in the quotation already given to 'culture values approved for', but not necessarily *by*, all members of society. It would be sufficient for Merton's theory if only a sizeable minority of the lower class (as well as other classes) had assimilated the goal.

It is customary and easy to refer to Merton's approach as a theory, but strictly speaking it is not. It does, however, provide a framework that begins to help us think about the connection between social problems and social structure, and Merton himself has been ready to modify his original ideas and to accept the modifications of others. He has recently suggested, for example, that chronic deviant behaviour probably constitutes the occasional and limiting case. The more usual situation of anomie would be one in which men, caught up in the disjunction between society and culture (or ends and means), may deviate from widely accepted standards in some of their activities, conform in others, and vacillate between these responses, unless they are involved in social responses which tend to consolidate their deviance. This suggestion of the importance of the response of a person's associates helps to remove a legitimate objection to the early formulation of Merton's approach; that it tended to be atomistic, depicting the individual as 'choosing' his adaptations in isolation from others.

Other sociologists have attempted to develop the anomic approach by suggesting modifications in the general 'theory' or by extending the categorisation of possible situations in which, to adapt a phrase of Durkheim, society is insufficiently present in individuals. Cloward, for example (Cloward, 1959, and Cloward and Ohlin, 1960), whilst accepting that access to the institutionalised means to generally approved goals is not available to every member of a society, has argued that access to the illegitimate means is also differentially distributed throughout the social structure. In a detailed consideration of Merton's categorisation of possible adaptations to goals and means, Dubin (1959) has outlined three important distinctions, between simple rejection (−) and rejection followed by substitution of alternative goals or norms (±), between the values guiding the selection of particular behaviour and the actual behaviour, and, finally, between institutionalised means (the actual behaviour of people) and institutionalised norms, which set the limits between which the means are prescribed. Thus, Dubin distinguishes between behavioural innovation and value innovation. Using the distinction between norms and means he can distinguish between the following kinds of deviant adaptation.

Type of Deviant Adaptation	Mode of Attachment to Cultural Goals	Institu-tional Norms	Institu-tional Means
1. *Behavioural Innovation*			
(a) Institutional Invention	+	±	±
(b) Normative Invention	+	±	+
(c) Operating Invention	+	+	±
2. *Value Innovation*			
(a) Intellectual Invention	±	+	+
(b) Organisation Invention	±	±	+
(c) Social Movement	±	+	±

The approach to social problems through the concept of anomie can, then, accommodate change and revision, and it does represent a substantial body of work that has developed since its early formulation in the writings of Durkheim. It is also, of course, open to criticism on a number of grounds. Criticism has usually referred to the lack of empirical evidence that might be used to test propositions that could be derived from the approach, and to faults in the analysis of the key terms and ideas.

In terms of the lack of supporting empirical evidence, for example, Lander and Lander suggest that existing evidence casts doubt on the ideas that the dream of success and the obligation to strive for top positions have been internalised in all strata of society. 'The quick surrender of working-class youth to the difficulties they face is not necessarily forced or unwilling. Their aspirations are controlled by a relatively objective appraisal of what is possible' (Lander and Lander, 1964). They report some unpublished research by Gold who found that delinquents tended to have lower aspirations than non-delinquents,

29

and tended also to be more confident of achieving their lower aspirations. In a similar vein Hyman (1954) has suggested that the lower-class individual does not want as much success as the middle-class person, knows he would not in any case achieve it, and does not want what would help him to achieve it. On the other hand, a sizeable proportion of the lower class do not share their own group's value system.

The criticism that urges the lack of supporting empirical evidence and the presence of evidence that appears contrary is worth consideration, but it is sometimes difficult to be sure what evidence might count against Merton's theory. The theory does not, as was emphasised earlier, depend on the internalisation of cultural goals at all strata of society, but it does demand, as Merton has pointed out, the internalisation in a sizeable proportion of the lower class. The question naturally arises, how large is 'sizeable'? This raises the serious problem of the difficulty of identifying a set of values that can be considered universal throughout a modern society. Can we use the idea of universal success goals, ask Lander and Lander, to explain the high delinquency rate amongst Negroes in the Southern States of America when it is highly unlikely that Southern whites foster the idea of common success goals? How does Merton's theory account for the wide variation in the prevalence of delinquency among working-class areas? Is it the anomic quality of an area rather than its economic characteristics that is fundamentally associated with the delinquency rate? In considering these and other criticisms it is important to note that social problems cannot be seen as direct results of anomie which can be in its turn directly observable. Anomie is a middle-distance concept which cannot be taken as something given in a situation; it describes rather a condition that is the product of identifiable sociological variables.

Criticism has also been made of Merton's analysis of social reality. It has been suggested, for instance, that his central distinction between cultural goals and institutional means attempts to separate elements that are essentially linked. Lemert (Clinard *et al.* 1964) has argued that the distinction cannot easily be made in practice. In his view there are no values that always constitute ends and values that always constitute means. He suggests that in America the excessive pursuit of money could be described simply as a concentration on means at the expense of ends. Lemert sees social reality as a complex of changing social associations which combine and separate in different ways. The relationships between groups in a society can be based on separatism, federation, tenuous accommodation and perhaps open alliance. Society, argues Lemert, is not built on the value consensus that is to be found in Merton, and enables him to separate so readily means and ends, and to identify deviance with such clarity.

Summary

In this chapter we have considered the general ways in which sociologists have approached social problems. Sociologists have used different theoretical approaches, and have differed in the importance they have given to the study of social problems and the extent to which they have attempted to connect this study with more general sociological theory. Amongst the numerous and differing approaches two have been selected for special attention, the 'process' approach and the 'structural'. Neither answers all questions about the general origins of social problems, but each makes an important contribution towards a general theory of social problems. Sociologists have also helped to clarify some elements in our general theorising about these problems, by suggesting that it will be systematically influenced by our general model of society (whether we choose an integration or a conflict model or move between these positions according to the problem we are investigating), and that behind a persistent choice of either model may be concealed a more basic ideological position.

3
Sociology and crime

The size and shape of the problem

Of all the contemporary social problems it is perhaps crime that attracts most public interest and concern. The reasons for this are complex, reflecting, amongst other factors, a disappointment that the reduction of poverty has not produced the kind of social solidarity that was at one time, perhaps naïvely, expected. It is not only that the total volume of crime at any one point in a society's life causes concern, but that the shape and size of the different kinds of crime indicates a very complex social problem. Serious crime has increased, as have crimes committed by children and young persons. Between 1938 and 1962 the number of indictable crimes known to the police in England and Wales increased from over 283,000 per annum to over 896,000, whilst non-indictable offences increased in the same period from over 709,000 to about 1,063,000. The numbers convicted of crimes of violence increased over the same period from nearly 1,600 to nearly 12,000, and of sex offences from about 2,300 to about 6,000. Offences by children and by young people show a similar increase in the total number of offences committed annually and in the more serious crimes.

In dealing with these and similar figures, however, the sociologist appreciates that he must interpret them as products of law-enforcing agencies. This is certainly the case if he sees as his preliminary task the establishment of some idea of the 'true' size and shape of the problem he must then proceed to explain. It is also the case if he adopts another possible basis for his research, and emphasises that what is of importance is not an estimate of the 'true', 'abstract' position, but the social reactions to this particular form of deviance. This is so because he will need to establish some contrasts between the kinds of deviance that the social agencies treat in different ways and the kinds that somehow or other escape detection or treatment. Just as the sociologist in the field of mental health must both see and see beyond the psychiatric conceptions of behaviour and the statistics produced by the health agencies, so the sociologist in crime must study and also interpret the statistics of crime.

There are many sources of distortion in the criminal statistics and several ways in which an interpretation may go astray. The statistics were not originally conceived with research in mind: the legal categories involved actually mask differences that are of importance to those who wish to study the size and the shape of the problem. The division of offences into indictable (with the possibility of trial by jury) and non-indictable (without this choice) divides what is often the same broad type of offence into two separate categories. The non-indictable offences are often considered less serious than the others, but exclusive preoccupation with indictable offences can produce a false picture. Power (1962), for instance, has shown that the non-indictable offences amongst juveniles include those that currently cause social concern—

34

malicious damage, carrying an offensive weapon, various assaults on the police etc. His study in East London, based on every boy and girl between 8 and 16 living in the area and appearing before a juvenile court, indicated the peak age was not 14, as assumed by those looking only at the statistics relating to indictable offences. In fact, apart from a slight dip at 15, numbers increased each year and were still rising at 16. An examination of the actual offences committed by the juveniles revealed the existence of two fairly distinct patterns. The first, which rose sharply until the age of 14 and fell away, was connected with one of the many forms of stealing. The second, which was scarcely apparent until 13 years of age and then rose until 16 and apparently continued, was largely associated with what could be broadly described as hooliganism.

This is an example of the consequences of the faulty interpretation of statistics based on legal categories. Faulty interpretation can also arise from the fact that the law-enforcing agencies are themselves open to all the influences that impinge on the institutions and groups of a society at any time. These influences change and it is such changes that may be reflected in the annual statistics rather than a change in the forms of social behaviour that the statistics should show. Thus, changes in the level of tolerance from one period to another may influence the statistics, as will differences in the efficiency and strength of the police force and so on. Criminal behaviour by members of some groups in society will, because of their position within the structure of that society, be more visible to law-enforcing agencies. It has, for instance, been suggested that the characterisation of crime as predominantly a lower working-class phenomenon is due to the greater visibility of the general actions of this group. Comment has also been made about the ease with which

possibly middle-class criminologists could persuade themselves and others that the large number of motoring
offences (again, mainly non-indictable) were somehow
not really crimes (Wootton, 1959). (Incidentally, recent
work (Willett, 1964) questions whether motoring offenders
can properly be characterised as 'middle-class'.)

In spite, however, of these and other ways in which the
criminal statistics may be seriously misleading, it seems
to be established that they distort rather than totally mis-
represent the picture of crime today. We can assume
that the widespread concern at the increase in the volume
of crime is, in general, correctly based. What is the subject for discussion and investigation is the size of the
increase, and, perhaps of greater importance, the kind of
increase. The sociologist cannot be sure what changes
have to be explained before it has been established whether
the increase in crime is an increase in the number of
crimes (thus, the same number of criminals could be
becoming more criminal, i.e. committing more crimes)
or in the number of criminals. Of course these are not
mutually exclusive alternatives: some of the increase
could be the result of more recidivism, whilst some could
be produced by more first offenders.

It is not easy to answer this question. The official
statistics give only a static annual picture of the total
amount of crime committed each year. A cumulative
idea of the total number of criminals (those who have
been convicted at least once) at any one time cannot be
readily obtained. The statistics record the incidence of
crime (the number of new criminal acts known to the
police within a particular time span) and what we require
for the solution of this present problem is an accurate
assessment of the prevalence of crime (the total number
of the population who have committed crime at any one
point in time). It is, however, possible to calculate a

prevalence rate for recorded delinquency, and Little (1965 (a); 1965 (b)) concludes that in relation to adolescent offenders the increase in crime can be explained in the following terms: 28% of the increase is due to population increase; 42% to the increase in rates of first offenders; 6% to the recidivism of the additional first offenders, and 24% to increased rates of recidivism (Little, 1965 (b)). In general he suggests that prevalence figures are far higher than the annual incidence figures, and that they show the same kind of difference between the rates for males and those for females as the incidence statistics. A substantial minority of the male population is officially delinquent by their 21st birthday. In view of this the problem to be explained by the sociologist is the increase in first offenders, and the smaller increase in, and indeed the existence of, the repeated offence. The occurrence of an officially delinquent act may be of less importance both sociologically and from the point of view of society than a delinquent career.

Sociological factors

On the whole, sociologists, whilst giving proper weight to the critical discussion of criminal statistics, have not given much attention to the explanation of the changes they suggest in the volume of crime. Rather their pre-occupation has been with elucidating sociological factors accounting for the occurrence and for the continuance of crime in our industrialised society. It is now possible to find, particularly in the United States, a fairly considerable theoretical contribution to the sociological understanding of crime. Much of this is at a quite high level of abstraction and awaits empirical testing. British studies are perhaps stronger on the empirical side (see e.g. Morris, 1957; Mays, 1954), but Downes (1966) has recently published a study which includes a considerable amount of useful theoretical discussion. Before considering the studies so far made there are three general observations to be put.

Firstly, the problem to be explained is taken to be that of working-class criminality. Some criminologists certainly have focused our attention on the middle-class criminal (Sutherland, 1949), but there is fairly general agreement that the problem is still similar to that described earlier by Mayhew who saw crime as essentially a social phenomenon perpetuated by anti-social attitudes and ways of behaving which were transferred from generation to generation in an environment characterised by poverty, bad housing and economic insecurity. Yet crimes are committed by members of other classes who live in apparently favourable environments. This, too, must find a place in a sociological explanation of crime, but sometimes the middle-class delinquent, particularly the juvenile, is treated as a residual category to be explained primarily in terms of psychological disturbance. To adapt the words of an old song, 'it's the poor what gets the sociological explanation, the rich the psychological'.

Secondly, a sociological explanation of crime must meet a number of exacting criteria. Studies in the past have often been partial, failing to recognise that, as Cloward and Ohlin (1960) have persuasively argued, a sociological theory of crime must attempt to answer five important questions. These questions, which could and should be asked of each kind of deviance, are:

(a) what is the precise nature of the delinquent adaptation to be explained;
(b) how is this mode of adaptation distributed throughout the social structure;
(c) to what problems might this pattern of adjustment be a response;

(d) why is one particular mode of delinquency chosen in contrast to another;

(e) what determines the relative stability or instability of a particular pattern of delinquency.

Thirdly, whilst we speak of an approach towards a sociological theory of crime, it is possible to identify a number of different answers given by sociologists to the question, why crime? A psychological approach can include such studies as those by Trasler (1962), based on learning theory, and by Friedlander (1947), based on psychoanalytic ideas. Similarly, sociologists do not present an agreed syllabus for the investigation and understanding of delinquency. Amongst sociological explanations of crime can be found in the course of the development of the subject the ecological hypothesis, and, developing from this along more precisely sociological lines, various attempts to explain what has been termed the delinquent sub-culture. This has been seen as a more or less straightforward reflection of the lower-class way of life, as the expression of values implicit in the general life of a society, though not recognised, or as a solution to the problem of adjustment presented by the lower-class members' place in the structure of the society: for some the problem is primarily that of status, for others it is that of frustrated social and economic advancement. Each of these ideas is worth considering in some detail.

The ecological view

The ecological approach affirms that a relationship exists between people who share a locality and that this relationship is connected to the physical character of the environment, i.e. its railway tracks, canals, main roads, and such features as land use. This approach originated in Chicago in the late 1910's and the 1920's and is associated with the names Park (1952), Thraser (1927), and Shaw (1929). The social ecologists advanced a theory of urban growth which emphasised the zonal development of a city. Park and others (1925), for example, saw the growth of Chicago in terms of five zones: the central business district, a zone of transition (rooming houses, brothels etc.), working men's homes, residential flats and single family dwellings, and, finally, respectable suburbia. The city developed, they thought, through a process of change expressed in terms of invasion—dominance—succession as new populations came and departed. Originally the whole population of the city lived around the central business district but as new commercial enterprises developed the wealthier inhabitants moved out; this led to a decrease in rentals which attracted the poor immigrants but encouraged the respectable artisans to move out of the central business area. The artisans in their turn tended to displace the wealthy who consequently moved into the suburbs.

Within these zones were to be found what the ecologists called 'natural areas'. For some of these theorists these were essentially unplanned products of a city's physical growth, based on a framework of transportation, business organisations, parks etc. For others—and here we find a departure from a strictly ecological view—these areas were predominantly cultural, made up of populations of certain races, incomes etc. Certain natural areas which produced an unexpectedly high rate of delinquency over a period of time in which there was a fairly rapid turnover in population were studied by Shaw (1929) and Shaw and McKay (1942). Their characterisation as delinquency areas marked an important stage in the development of criminology, even though, as Morris has pointed out (1957), the concept refers ambiguously to areas that produce delinquents and those in which a high number of delinquent acts occur. The ecology theory certainly over-emphasised the influence of the purely physical aspects of the environment, but these can have a place in a socio-logical theory if we look at the environment in terms of what it 'says' to the inhabitants concerning their valuation by other groups in society. However, it remains true that the emphasis in sociology has moved away from the physical features of an environment towards a closer investigation of social relations within the delinquent sub-culture and, in varying degrees, between the sub-culture and the cultures of other groups and institutions in the society.

The idea of a delinquent sub-culture

Cohen (1955), in an influential book, first used the idea of a delinquent sub-culture to explain certain forms of delinquency. Critics have not always noted that he was not attempting a general explanation of delinquency. He used the term to refer to a way of life that was traditional among gangs of young males, and this way of life repre-sented a common solution to problems they shared because of their position in the structure of society. As working-class male adolescents who lived in large towns and cities their common problems of adjustment arose through problems of status. The working-class boy could not avoid experiencing the pressures of, and succumbing to the in-fluence of, the predominant Protestant Ethic in our society, which stresses individual effort and achievement rather than social solidarity. He is in fact socialised almost against his will through institutions dominated by the middle class, of which the school is the most important. Yet because of limited opportunities he cannot attain status in middle-class contexts. This creates a problem of adjustment to which the delinquent sub-culture is a solution. For this sub-culture legitimises his conduct in so far as it represents a reversal of the norms of middle-class society. Thus, Cohen sees the sub-culture as possessing a number of characteristics that mark it off not only as distinct from, but also in conflict with, the wider society. The activities of the sub-culture are often non-utilitarian, malicious and negativistic, and the gang seems committed to short-term pleasure in a variety of forms. It is this versatility which, according to Cohen, accounts for the absence of girls, whose delinquency is largely restricted to theft and sexual misbehaviour.

Later Cohen (Cohen and Short, 1958) argued that there were in fact different kinds of delinquent sub-culture. The sub-culture outlined above was referred to as the 'parent male sub-culture' and it was considered that this sub-culture was carried by gangs and cliques of adolescents throughout the working class. This parent sub-culture gives birth to three variants, the conflict-orientated sub-culture, engaging predominantly in gang-warfare, the drug-addict sub-culture and that of the semi-professional thief. These variants on a common sub-cultural theme closely parallel the ideas put forward by Cloward and Ohlin (1960), on the conflict, the retreatist and the criminal sub-cultures. Each of these sub-cultures, according to Cloward and Ohlin, has particular values, beliefs and norms. Thus, the conflict sub-culture prescribes violence, the members believe their territory is surrounded by enemies, and value 'heart' and courage. The retreatist sub-culture, on the other hand, prescribes the illicit use of drugs, believes that the world about them is populated by 'squares', and values 'the kick'. It is important, however, to note that the delinquent sub-culture or its variant is not the only response open to the working-class boy in his difficulties in expressing middle-class values and achieving middle-class goals. Cohen refers to two other responses, those of the stable 'corner boy' who gives up the fight and the 'college boy' who plays 'the middle-class status game'.

These references to the work of Cohen, and of Cloward and Ohlin, give some idea of the main features of the concept, and also suggest some of the difficulties in using it. If, for example, we designate a set of beliefs, norms and attitudes as a sub-culture, what is the relationship between this sub-group and the wider society? This involves a consideration of one of the most changeable terms in sociology, culture. Firth (1947, p. 22), for instance, sees culture as the way of life of an organised set of individuals, but does this apply to any organised set? Are we correct in speaking, as we often do, of the culture of a factory, a school, or even of a family? If we are correct, are these separate cultures part of a common way of life or *sub*-cultures? Perhaps reference to a 'common way of life' is an overtly persuasive term which leads us to neglect the fact that most ways of life, like most individuals, contain important contradictions. The idea of a sub-culture embodies one possible contradiction, but where does a culture end and a sub-culture begin? If we think of a sub-culture not so much as a variant on a common theme, but as a possible substitute way of life, then the concept of a contraculture may prove more useful and expressive (Yinger, 1960).

If these are some of the difficulties that are to be found in the concept of the sub-culture, is the idea worth using? Certainly, its value has been questioned (Wootton, 1959), and it will not provide an explanation for all delinquency: some problems of social living are not capable of a subcultural solution. In our society it appears in general easier for men to adopt such a solution than for women. Yet human problems are not distributed randomly throughout the social structure, and our problems must be solved in a way that leaves our standing with our reference groups unimpaired. Those sharing the problems deriving from our need to achieve the respect of our fellows gravitate more closely together and as a solution tend to develop new criteria for status.

Why might the delinquent sub-culture arise? As previously indicated, a number of solutions have been proposed for this problem. These will be discussed in some detail.

Lower-class life itself as the milieu for gang delinquency.

This view, associated with W. B. Miller in the United States (1958) and Mays in Britain (1954), helps us to see that one of the main difficulties in the study of any way of life is to dispense with our own preconceptions. Miller argues that we should attempt to see lower-class culture as a long-established way of life with its own integrity. He describes this culture as a way of life revolving around what he calls 'focal concerns'. These are identified as: (a) concern about '*trouble*'; law-abiding behaviour is valued explicitly but in some cases law-violating behaviour is covertly valued; (b) *toughness*, due, suggests Miller, to the fact that a significant proportion of lower-class males are reared in households dominated by women, often because of the absence of a regular father-figure; (c) *smartness*, in the sense of being 'one up' on other people; (d) *excitement*, to be found mainly in drinking, adventuring with sex and aggression, though these kinds of activity alternate with periods of quiescence and inactivity; (e) *fate*, shown in the reliance on luck, omens etc.; (f) *autonomy*, with an overt emphasis on independence but with a covert tendency towards dependence. A culture which revolves around these focal concerns generates a milieu that is conducive to gang delinquency.

How successful is this interpretation? It certainly

attempts to see lower-class culture in its own right, but
we need to ask how far such a culture in fact exists in
its own right without being influenced by essentially
invidious comparisons with other sub-cultures or the
general culture. In other words, the theory pays in-
sufficient attention to the social relationships between
the members of different sub-cultures. In so far as Miller
sees conflict between the lower-class culture and the
middle-class-dominated legal system—and we must here
recall his concern with implicit as well as explicit elements in the focal concerns—it is an external conflict
between individuals who espouse different value systems.
Other theorists would argue that the conflict should be
seen as internalised. Cohen, for instance, used the concepts of ambivalence and reaction formation, emphasising that the delinquent's problem was to find an adaptation to an internalised system of value.

Secondly, Miller sees the lower-class culture as a
distinctive cultural form, but there are variations in
behaviour and value amongst working-class people. There
are varieties of lower-class culture. Miller does refer to
the existence of 'sub-types of lower class-culture', but does
not develop this important idea. One way in which these
sub-types might be categorised has been suggested by
S. M. Miller (Riessman *et al.*, 1964). Using the two
measures of economic security/insecurity and family
stability/instability, he suggests a fourfold classification
into the stable poor, the strained poor, the copers and
the unstable. In Britain some attempts have been made to
use a distinction within traditional working-class life between 'the roughs' and the 'respectable' (Klein, 1965, Vol.
I). Whatever distinctions are adopted, it is important that
'working-class' and 'middle-class' life are not *assumed* to
be homogeneous. Statements about the relationship between delinquency and social class in both America and

Britain tend to move uneasily but often in an unnoticed manner between statements about the working class or lower class and those concerning the lower working class or a sub-type of the lower class.

One of the consequences of Miller's rather global conception of the lower-class culture is that it leads him to over-emphasise the extent of the female-based household. One of the problems arising from such a household would inevitably be that of masculine identification. Miller sees this as particularly a working-class problem (see also Spinley, 1954), whereas Cohen uses the mother-centred family to explain specifically middle-class delinquency. Possibly, this kind of family is to be found throughout the social structure.

Finally, we should deepen our empirical knowledge of any particular sub-culture. The concept of 'focal concerns' is useful, but we must be sure that it is actually organising material that is directly descriptive of the behaviour of the people concerned. This is not to support the view that only behaviour can be observed, but it is to suggest that at the present stage of investigation we should use carefully the kind of concept that lies midway between empirical fact and general theory. Neither should we neglect the historical approach in our interpretation of the empirical material. If, for example, we do find an extensive reliance on omens etc., this could be seen as a rather quaint survival, but it is more likely to be a reflection of the fact that for years 'the working class' has been unable to predict and make provision for its future, since this has been in the control of others or of natural forces.

Delinquency as the expression of subterranean values

This view sees delinquency as the expression of values in the wider society that are not openly acknowledged. Upholders of this view, unlike Miller who supposes that the working-class child has internalised only working-class norms, argue that the delinquent's problem is to neutralise his guilt reactions on violating or contemplating the violation of the acknowledged social norms. Sykes and Matza (1957) suggest that the delinquent in fact often experiences guilt, respects 'the really honest person', and distinguishes clearly between those who can be 'legitimately' victimised and those who cannot. The delinquent, in order to pave the way for acts of non-conformity, uses what are described as 'techniques of neutralisation' which help him to meet the demands of conformity. As examples of such techniques the authors suggest the following: denial of responsibility; denial that his acts actually injure people; denial of the victim, as in assaults on minority groups who 'do not really matter'; condemnation of those who enforce the norms ('the police are corrupt'); and the appeal to higher loyalties ('I did not do it for myself').

Such techniques are undoubtedly used, but, as Downes points out (1966), the theory does not explain why they are so much needed at the lower end of the social hierarchy. Sykes and Matza see the delinquent not so much as a deviant but as a person who expresses the values of a leisured *élite*—the emphasis on daring, the rejection of the ordinary discipline of work, the emphasis on luxury, and the respect paid to masculinity shown in the use of force. This approach, however, does not account for the social class distribution of delinquency, since the attractiveness of delinquency and the appeal of the techniques of neutralisation which make it possible are presumably spread equally throughout the society. The contrast between acknowledged and subterranean values, like Miller's between the explicit and implicit aspects of the focal concerns of a culture, is of interest, as is the emphasis on the 'fun' and 'attractiveness' of much delinquent activity. Yet, as Downes has stated (1966), the authors have failed to develop the implications that arise from the considerable differences in the distribution of leisure amongst adolescents: the lower working-class boy cannot easily attain the leisure goals fostered by the commercial world for the 'benefit' of the adolescent.

Delinquency as the solution of a problem

Delinquency as a phenomenon associated with groups of adolescent working-class males has been seen by Cohen (1955) and by Cloward and Ohlin (1960) as a solution to certain problems of adaptation facing individuals in a particular position in the social structure. It is not the only possible solution, but one that attains considerable significance. Cohen sees the problem primarily in terms of status. The lower working-class male cannot achieve status within a middle-class context. He therefore seeks status according to an alternative system by participating in groups in which activities are legitimised precisely because they are contradictory to middle-class norms. Cloward and Ohlin give more emphasis to aspirations within lower-class society. The legitimate means to satisfy these are not open to every member of the lower class and those whose aspirations are frustrated seek illegitimate means to reach them. This thesis is, of course, basically that of Merton (1957). Cloward and Ohlin, however, extend this by questioning whether the illegitimate means to socially sanctioned goals are available to all, irrespective of their social position. They argue that illegal alternatives are only available relatively, and that the rather global notion of the delinquency area as 'disorganised' fails to distinguish between different degrees of disorganisation which give rise to opportunities for different kinds of delinquent career. Kobrin has suggested that delinquency areas show important differences in the degree to which integration between the criminal and conventional systems is achieved (1951).

These are important theories because they stress the effect on social relations of interaction between cultural groups and the significance of the delinquent norm and the delinquent career. Yet, like most theories in this field, they are not free from difficulty. Bordua, for example (1962), supports the 'classical' view of the gang propounded by Thrasher (1936), who saw the delinquent subculture as a way of life that would develop as a by-product of the process of a group becoming a gang, rather than seeing the gang as the kind of group that would develop if boys deliberately set about creating a delinquent subculture. Other critics question Cohen's characterisation of gang behaviour as malicious and negativistic. Kitsuse and Dietrick, for instance (1959), suggest that middle-class groups may behave in this way, but working-class gangs do not. Others question the prevalence of the structured gang, or whether their aggressive acts are predominantly directed against middle-class targets. Finally, it could be argued that special features in American society account for the kind of gang life theories attempt to explain.

In British work on this subject certainly most of the evidence supports Miller's view that the major part of delinquency represents adolescent conformity to the expectations of lower-class culture. The most recent by Downes, however, advances the application of sub-cultural delinquency in this country. His study of East London showed an unintegrated slum area where crime tends to be individualistic, unorganised and not an alternative avenue of advancement for those who are socially mobile in an upward direction. Gangs, in the sense of groups in which delinquency is a central norm, hardly exist. How-

ever, the process that leads the lower-class boy into delinquency is one of dissociation from the middle-class-dominated contexts of school, work and recreation. This dis-
enchantment provokes an over-emphasis on leisure goals,
which the lower-class boy needs to achieve, but cannot
readily do so. He reacts to this frustration by reaffirming
the working-class value system. Yet in this system the
old leisure values have lost their attractiveness and
potency, and the delinquent sub-culture is seen as an
alternative.

4
Sociology and mental illness

The size and shape of the problem

Any attempt to estimate the size and delineate the shape of the social problem of mental illness meets the difficulty that the condition we see and investigate has already been subject to a number of different social processes : it has, for varying periods of time, been treated *as* madness, even if the condition has not been treated *for* madness. Cases are defined as mentally ill by a range of people applying different criteria, for example doctors, neighbours, relatives etc. In each group varying attitudes will influence what is considered a mental illness, what is considered a less serious instance of 'emotional disturbance' to which we might all be subject at one time or another, and what is considered eccentricity, amiable or otherwise. Unless we undertake to screen whole communities through psychiatric examination we cannot be sure about the prevalence of mental illness in any area, and even this will not tell us the size of the *problem* of mental illness, since this will depend, in part at least, on prevailing attitudes. The same kind of difficulty is met, of course, in the study of crime, where only identified crime can be investigated. However, undetected crime is still crime, but undetected mental illness may not be by definition a problem. So much will depend on the definitions of all concerned, whereas the definition of a crime is much less variable.

If this is the kind of difficulty facing the study of the size of the contemporary problem of mental illness, clearly the investigation of changes in the size of the problem over the years will be much more hazardous. It is frequently suggested that what is termed the increase in the pace of life has resulted in a considerable increase in the numbers of the population who become mentally ill. We certainly have witnessed in Great Britain a considerable recent increase in the numbers admitted to mental hospital. Between 1949 and 1960 annual admissions rose, by 59,000, from 55,000 to 114,000. Admission rates rose by about 50%, and, with the exception of children and adolescents, the increase has been fairly evenly spread throughout the age groups. Yet we must see this increase against a background of changes in our social policy in regard to mental hospital admission and treatment. It is now clear that the hospital is not, for many patients at any rate, a place which it is very difficult to leave: between 1951 and 1960 male discharges increased by 117% and female by 128%. Periods of treatment in hospital are now very much shorter. These changes both reflect and encourage changes in our general attitudes towards the mentally ill, and because of these and other changes it is difficult to know whether there has been an increase in the true incidence of mental illness or a change in the use and deployment of the hospital services.

Figures for patients admitted to hospital, however, refer to only one aspect of the size of the problem of mental illness. There is a great deal of such illness which, for a variety of reasons, never reaches the hospital, and it can-

not be assumed that it is always the least 'serious' conditions that are kept out. Watts *et al.* (1964) concluded
from their survey of serious mental illness in 261 general
practices in Great Britain that for every person hospitalised
for a mental disorder there were 2 seriously disturbed
patients receiving treatment outside the hospital. Turning
to psychiatric morbidity in general, estimates of the size
of the problem in the community vary considerably. Kessel
and Shepherd (1962) suggested that the estimates of general
practitioners tended to vary with their theoretical orientation. Thus, doctors who stressed organic factors in
mental illness rarely gave a figure above 10% when esti-
mating the psychiatric morbidity in their practice; those
who thought in terms of stress conditions and psycho-
somatic complaints gave a figure of 20%, whilst those
who adhered to psychoanalytic theorising gave the highest
figure, 40%.

These figures and estimates are concerned, of course,
with the mentally ill or the hospitalised mentally ill in
general. Are there any distinctions to be drawn between
the different social categories of people who become
mentally ill, so that we can begin to discern, even in rather
blurred outline, the shape of the problem? Three social
variables have been particularly studied: the contrast
between urban and rural rates of diagnosed mental illness;
factors of nationality or culture, largely in connection
with movement within and between countries; and, lastly,
socio-economic variables. Leacock, in a useful review of
some of the main studies of these variables (ed. Leighton
et al., 1957), questions the consistency of the relationship
between high rates of mental illness in urban areas and
low rates in the rural. Figures from a Norwegian survey,
for example, showed no such relationship. Only Oslo had
far higher rates than the other areas, both urban and rural,
and this could probably be explained in terms of the con-

siderable drift of population to the city. It was suggested that the higher incidence in urban areas found in several other studies was due to the fact that psychotics were more easily observed in the city and consequently more readily hospitalised. On the other hand, it can be argued that odd behaviour is less visible in the city and that in conditions of 'anonymity' action is less likely to be initiated. It is also necessary to explain, as Wardle has pointed out, the rural/urban differences in conditions other than the psychotic (1962).

Perhaps the important factor to be considered is not the comparatively straightforward identification of an area as urban or rural, but the quality of social life within its boundaries. Some sociologists use the idea of degrees of 'social integration' to identify such a quality. Others use the term 'social isolation'. One study, for example, showed a correlation between an area with high admission rates for schizophrenia and such indices of social isolation as comparative friendlessness, infrequent membership of organisations, more rented than owned accommodation and so on. This last criterion perhaps highlights the tendency to confuse descriptions of characteristics of an area which apply more or less to all its inhabitants and statements that describe the minority of the mentally ill in whom we are especially interested. Wardle (1962) illustrates this kind of difficulty by reference to areas in America with high rates of mental subnormality and also with a high proportion of foreign-born residents. This seemed to lead to the conclusion that foreigners tended to be less intelligent than the natives, but investigation on an individual basis showed that the foreigners had a higher average intelligence than that of the general population. Similarly, a study of mental illness suggested that the cluster of cases in the city centre was due to the residential pattern of a minority of the sample who were single, divorced or separated men (quoted Leacock 1957). In other words we should distinguish between facets of the life of an area and factors that might lead people to take up residence within its boundaries.

Of all the conditions or groups of condition identified by psychiatrists as mental illness schizophrenia seems to have attracted most attention from the sociologists. Perhaps this is because it is, individually and collectively, a crippling disease or because, whatever the difficulties of psychiatric diagnosis—and these are notorious—it is more readily recognised than, for example, some of the neurotic states. Whatever the reason, it has been given special attention. In studies of schizophrenia and migration, for example, it has been found that it is more prevalent amongst those who have recently moved from one community to another than amongst the host population or the community recently left. Yet it does not seem that this can admit of a simple explanation. Are those in whom the illness is incipient restless, unsettled people? Øedogaard (1936), for example, distinguished between those moving within Norway, those migrating outside Norway and those moving into the city. He suggested that movement within the country was some kind of logical next step for the capable and ambitious man, whilst the seaport and far-away places tended to attract the restless people, without family or friendly connections. Alternatively, is it the process of acculturation which produces the strains leading to mental illness? Malzberg (1940) analysed the figures for mental illness into those in the native-born children of foreign parents and those in the native-born children of one native and one foreign parent. It was the second group that was responsible for the high rate of mental illness amongst the second generation. On the other hand, their high rate of illness was composed to a considerable extent of the psychoses of old age.

Social class factors

The social variable that has been most frequently studied, particularly in recent years, is the socio-economic. The relevance of social class to the incidence and the prevalence of mental illness, mainly in the case of schizophrenia, has been studied in both Britain and America. In using this material cumulatively, however, differences between the criteria (and probably also the definition) of social class should be recognised. Hollingshead and Redlich (1958), for instance, use a combined index of class, consisting of education, occupation and place of residence, and this prevents them from investigating the influence of any one of these factors in relationship with any other. Does the level of education within each occupational group affect the propensity to define one's problems as psychological? However, what is of more immediate relevance is the fact that differences between their findings that 91% of the schizophrenic patients were in the same social class as their family orientation (e.g. 89% of their lower working-class patients came from lower working-class families), and those of Goldberg and Morrison (that the fathers of schizophrenic patients represented a typical cross-section of the community in which they lived) can be explained, partly at least, in terms of the different criteria of class adopted in the two surveys.

Most of the evidence shows an uneven class distribution in patients diagnosed schizophrenic. Hollingshead and Redlich, for instance, give the following index of the prevalence of the illness, in which 100 would be scored by a social class showing the same proportion of schizophrenics as it itself comprises of the general population :

Class I   22
Class II   33

Class III   43
Class IV   88
Class V   246

From this it can be seen that whilst differences in prevalence rates vary from class to class the difference between class IV and V is very striking. Stein (1957), in a study of first admissions for schizophrenia from two socially contrasted sets of London boroughs, found a social gradient in the inception as well as the prevalence of the illness. In America Clausen (1959) is one of the few investigators to find no inverse relationship between rates of schizophrenia and socio-economic status. He suggests that the reason for this may be found in the fact that his study, unlike others, was of a *small* urban community and that the signficance of social status differences depends on the social framework in which they have evolved. Stein makes a similar point, suggesting that the use of occupation as an index of social class in areas of different status or different traditions is open to criticism.

The high rate of diagnosed schizophrenia in the unskilled working class is certainly more firmly established than the connection between class and other illnesses, or between class and mental illness in general. There seems to be some tendency for manic-depression to be associated with the middle class, but this is by no means established. Hollingshead and Redlich (1958) put forward the theory of an inverse relationship between social class and mental illness; the lower the social class the higher the rate of mental illness. Yet, as Miller and Mishler point out (1964), this is not fully borne out by their figures. They have successfully established a difference between class V and the other classes, but by concentrating on their prevalence data they fail to give proper emphasis to the fact that class IV has the lowest overall rate of mental illness.

The contribution of the sociologist

There seem to be at least four ways in which the sociologist might contribute to the study of mental illness. Firstly, he has recently become interested in studying the kinds of fact already mentioned : those social relationships that influence the process whereby people define themselves and are defined by others as 'mad', as 'patients', and as 'ex-patients' who are 'improved' or 'cured'; the social relations within the specialised organisations that 'treat' the patient, and the relationship between personnel, patients, organisation and policies. This is an important area of study, and some would restrict sociologists to investigations within its confines, since they find the sociological contribution to the study of the causation of mental illness so meagre (Wardle, 1962).

Others remain convinced that a study of social relations will shed some light on the causation of mental illness, and it should be said that this has not yet been investigated with sufficient rigour to admit of a definite answer as to the extent of the contribution to be expected from sociology. It is clearly a field of importance. Are there features of the social structure that might account for the distribution of at least one major mental illness along class lines? Laing (1962) has stated that not all who would can be psychotic. This was primarily a psychological observation, but a similar kind of sociological limitation could be envisaged. It is not simply that, as Cohen has stated, 'Psychosis is, to oversimplify the matter, a way of solving certain kinds of problems; and, as in the case of most problems, the members of any society have a limited number of ways of solving them. . . . As a result, there are a limited number of ways in which a person can become psychotic' (1961, p. 470). As research in the field of delinquency suggests, ways of solving problems are not randomly distributed throughout the social structure : there may be limited ways in which a person in a particular class of a society can become psychotic.

Thirdly, sociologists and others have begun to face the problems arising from the fact that the human behaviour they wish to study comes to them, as it were, in borrowed clothes, comprising the categories of psychiatric illness. Can the sociologist re-describe the behaviour in terms more suited to his own understanding of the behaviour? If he can it is likely that the benefits will not be confined to his own discipline.

Finally, some sociological studies have been made of the ways in which the personnel of the services devoted to mental illness and mental disturbance describe their help and its objectives. Many of the innovations in recent years have arisen from and been justified by the Mental Health Movement (e.g. the child guidance clinic in the U.S.A. and Great Britain). This Movement encouraged people to think of mental health as a condition of well-being (variously but always most vaguely defined) and not simply the absence of mental illness. Conditions which had previously been considered 'bad' were now to be seen as symptoms of an illness. The literature of the Movement is as considerable as its influence, but the validity of this influence has been questioned in the sociological analysis of the literature.

Each of these four areas of potential and actual contribution by sociological study will now be considered in more detail.

The study of therapeutic organisations

The study of therapeutic organisations (those which are entitled to describe themselves as treating the mentally ill) starts with the investigation of those relationships and processes whereby people begin to think of themselves as 'mad', and are so defined by their relatives, friends and neighbours. It has been argued, for example, that a family with a mentally ill member can be seen and sees itself as part of a minority, with feelings of under-privilege and marginality. The family lives in an environment which must consist of many unknown reactions from others as well as expected and experienced social distance. The family engages in a number of defensive tactics : it attempts concealment, and interprets ambiguous social contacts as rejection. Gradually, it may come to accept the negative evaluation of others, but this is often an ambivalent acceptance which exists side by side with the search for other groups with the same characteristics and experience as theirs (ed. Clausen, 1955).

These kinds of social process do not, of course, occur in a vacuum; they are always related in some way to the kind of services of help that are available, which in turn reflect more general attitudes and beliefs. In the study of the services at the stage when the person sees himself, or his relatives are beginning to see him, as at least a potential patient particular attention has been given to the social class factor. Hollingshead and Redlich, for example (1958), found that the different forms of 'treatment' were not distributed randomly amongst patients in New Haven. The social class proportion of cases in custodial care (no treatment) increased markedly as one moved from the higher to the lower social strata, as did the proportion of cases receiving some form of organic treatment. In the case of patients receiving psychotherapy, on the other hand, the opposite progression was at work. It appears, then, that different treatments 'attract' different social classes. Other studies confirm that a relationship exists between a patient's social class and whether he is accepted for therapy (Myers and Schaffer, 1954), but there seems to be no agreement that there is also a relationship between a patient's class and the training and experience of the therapist to whom he is assigned (ed. Riessman, 1964). In the case of the treatment of mentally disturbed children the influence of class factors is less obvious, though it is still apparent (Maas, 1955).

However, where social class appears to be an important determinant of the kind of treatment given to the mentally ill and disturbed, we shall have to explain the force of its influence. It has been suggested that working-class patients approach a doctor with the expectation that they will be given some concrete form of treatment or, at least, told what to do. They are disappointed if they are offered a form of psychotherapy, and react by failing to keep further appointments. They then either deteriorate to a condition which demands custody, or eventually find someone who will give them the treatment they expect. Yet empirical research questions this explanation, showing that in fact the new patient from the working class does expect that psychiatric issues will be raised and discussed, and that the doctor will take a moderately non-directive role (ed. Riessman, 1964). Other investigators see the comparative absence of the working class from the ranks of those experiencing psychotherapy as a result of the different speech systems used by the middle-class therapist and the working-class client (Bernstein, 1964).

A 'patient' can be admitted to a wide range of therapeutic organisations. He can be accepted for treatment on the basis of an hour or so each week in a child guidance clinic or he can be a resident patient in what Goffman (1961) has described, graphically if not always clearly, as a 'total institution'. Goffman, in using this term, wishes to draw our attention to a number of different institutions (hospitals, prisons, monasteries etc.) which share the following characteristics : the normal separation of places of work, sleep and play is broken down, life in a 'total institution' is lived in the same place; each phase of activity within the institution is carried out in the immediate company of a large group of others, all of whom are treated alike; all phases of the day's activities are tightly scheduled and rationally organised. Yet, whatever the structure of the therapeutic organisation and whatever its objectives and programmes, the person accepted as a patient has begun, at least, to learn to play a number of organisational roles *vis-à-vis* the different groups with whom he has contact. For the sociologist the hospital or clinic does not consist of two separate groups, patients and staff, who meet and interact only in periods defined as 'treatment' times. Thus, Stanton and Schwarz (1954), in one of the best known studies of 'hospital sociology', drew attention to the ways in which patient disturbance could be seen as a reaction to disagreement and disunity in the staff group.

Therapeutic organisations can be said to differ along a number of dimensions (size, kind of patient etc.), and of these perhaps one of the most important is that of objectives. Hospitals in this country have for some time been questioning their function as places of custody, and have begun to experiment with various kinds of milieu therapy. This attempt to see the whole hospital life as potentially therapeutic is a major innovation, and a recent sociological study of a British hospital carrying out a new programme raises some interesting questions about the place and function of what was termed the new ideology of the hospital (Rapaport, 1960). The study identified four main themes in the programme for treating psychopaths—rehabilitation through reality confrontation, democratisation, permissiveness and communalism. These elements of the treatment ideology embodied a protest against the existing conventional hospital system and also helped to unite staff from diverse social backgrounds. The individual tenets in the creed were never closely defined, but the vagueness had its advantages; in leaving many qualifications implicit it furthered consensus where solidarity was necessary to achieve the staff's goals. For example, a psychiatrist and a psychopath might agree that 'most doctors do not know enough about the emotional problems of working-class people', and still establish a relationship. If, however, all the implicit qualifications of this statement were immediately made explicit they might not be able to find a basis for even beginning the relationship.

Vagueness, however, also had its dangers. Slogans are never fully attainable. It was, for instance, neither possible nor desirable for all communications in a hospital to be free. If the slogans were taken literally, then, the result was a striking discrepancy between the ideal and the actual, which imposes on the staff the burden of apparent inconsistency. The principles embodied in the slogans furnished no criteria for judging between them in concrete situations, and tended to become goals in themselves rather than means to treatment. This process hindered the objective appraisal of the work and increased resistance to change.

The study also raised some interesting questions concerning the extent to which indoctrination in the hospital ideology helped the patient when he left the hospital and returned to the 'outside' world.

On leaving the hospital the 'patient' begins the third phase of his social career, for he leaves with some kind of label (cured, improved etc.) which carries expectations for himself and for others. Recent research in Britain suggests that the quality of social relations to which the patient returns may have an important bearing on his future as an 'ex-patient' who does or does not once again become a 'patient'.

Brown and Topping (1958) showed that schizophrenic patients who lived with their wives or parents had a higher re-admission rate than those going to live with brothers, sisters, or more distant kin or in lodgings. The risk of deterioration in clinical condition increased when prolonged contact with close relatives in the house was unavoidable. These results could not be entirely explained by the length or past severity of the illness nor by differences in clinical condition at time of discharge. A later study (Brown *et al.* 1962) attempted to investigate the influence of family life in more detail, using a scale of emotional involvement which endeavoured to measure five factors: emotion, hostility, and dominant behaviour expressed by key relative towards patient, and emotion and hostility expressed by patient towards the key relative. The results of the study confirmed the hypothesis that patients returning to a relative who showed high emotional involvement would deteriorate more frequently than patients returning to a relative showing low emotional involvement. This held whether patients returned to parents, wife or more distant kin. A second hypothesis, that if the patient did return to such a home a small degree of contact with relatives would reduce the frequency of deterioration, was confirmed only for patients who were moderately or severely disturbed on discharge.

Clearly we need more follow-up studies of this kind for all types of mental illness. Yet this approach to the study of the third phase of a deviant career should not be allowed to obscure a point of some sociological significance. In studying deviant behaviour we might emphasise both the deviant behaviour and the social reaction it evokes. Mental illness is obviously a condition that places individuals in an aggregate or potential group whose identity depends both on their behaviour and also on the responses of other members of their community to this behaviour. However, membership of this aggregate does not restrict the individual to being deviant only in ways that evoke a response from the community that identified him as mentally ill. In other words, the follow-up study may reveal different kinds of deviant behaviour, but these may not necessarily be 'part of' the patient's original deviance. The follow-up may show a number of inadequacies in a patient's performance, but they may not measure the amount of their mental sickness.

Sociological study of the 'causes' of mental illness

At present studies indicate that the problem to be explained is the preponderance of diagnosed schizophrenia amongst the unskilled working class. A number of tentative explanations have been offered. It has been argued that the schizophrenic is someone who has drifted into unskilled occupations or who has rather suddenly dropped into them. Alternatively, instead of emphasising occupation, some critics see the schizophrenic as a direct result of a deprived milieu : he has lived among surroundings that 'breed' schizophrenia. Morrison found (1959) a concentration of schizophrenics in the unskilled working class, but an investigation of the fathers of the patients showed that they were uniformly distributed throughout the social classes : the schizophrenics in this study appeared in unskilled manual occupations immediately after leaving school. Myers and Roberts (1959) present evidence to suggest that the disease arises in circumstances of social isolation, whilst Susser and Watson (1962) suggest that 'drift' might be a characteristic of patients who have been hospitalised for any chronic illness.

The most recent evidence presented in this country on these questions is that contained in a study by Goldberg and Morrison (1963). The study was divided into two parts: (a) a documentary investigation of material from the General Register Office, which receives a card giving certain data on every patient admitted to a mental hospital in England and Wales, and (b) a clinical study at two mental hospitals. The documentary study showed that schizophrenic patients, aged 25–34, were born into families with a social class distribution very similar to that of the population as a whole, but that the patients themselves were disproportionately in class V occupations. The clinical study was undertaken partly to be more sure of the diagnosis of schizophrenia, and partly to attempt to discover something of the process of 'drift' in individual cases into unskilled manual occupations. For example, are the families of schizophrenics subjected to conditions which make it likely that the working careers of the fathers will deteriorate later in life, so that in consequence they move into lower-class areas, thus limiting the opportunities of their children?

The findings showed that the fathers had, on the whole, fairly solid and successful work careers and that they worked steadily. The occupations of grandfathers, uncles and brothers of the patient showed a similar distribution to that of father, which were, on the whole, not abnormal for their area. So, how does it happen that nearly half of the patients who come from families with reasonable standards of economic and social security were in semi- or unskilled jobs before their first admission to hospital? There seems in fact to be an *individual* downward drift. The main evidence for this was the ability of schizophrenic patients to win places at grammar schools, though they ended up in semi- or unskilled jobs. The discrepancies in social performance between father and son could be mainly attributed to the disease process itself. Patients whose illness had an insidious onset at adolescence did not attain any professional or technical skill; those whose illness started acutely before admission *dropped* in social class shortly before admission; those who were mentally subnormal as well as schizophrenic achieved no level of skill at all.

The authors warn us specifically not to equate good occupational records with sound personal relationships and they promise a further report on the family relationships in their families. Work that has already been done suggests that this is an interesting field to explore *differentially*. Thus, Hollingshead and Redlich (1958) in a study which brings evidence against the drift hypothesis argue that the family situations of schizophrenics varied according to social class. In their class III families the dominant and ambitious mother stood out; whereas in class V families it was the aggressive and physically violent father, plus economic insecurity and the feeling of rejection. Class III patients felt a sense of failure because they could not live up to class norms.

We have seen some of the evidence which supports the idea of a drift downward in social status in the individual patient, but American studies suggest that there is a notable proportion of fathers of schizophrenics whose work careers indicate upward social mobility. Might not some of the 'strain' (to use a rather vague but not altogether useless term) on the family be due to this? In other words, is mobility a factor in mental illness irrespective of its direction? Mobility may lead to confusion about one's reference group (the group whose standards one accepts as one's own) and consequently about one's own identity. Perhaps downward mobility is the most disturbing in this respect, but the significance of mobility may differ in the different classes. Hollingshead and Redlich, for example, reported that in their class III schizophrenics had experienced the *most* upward mobility from the point of departure of their parents' achievement, neurotics had experienced less and normal controls even less. However, in class V schizophrenics and normals had the same social mobility relative to parental achievement and neurotics had a slightly higher mobility.

So we must explore the differential meaning of family relationships and of mobility for each of the social classes. It is also important that we are not too impressed by any apparent monolithic quality in social classes. The Registrar General's Occupational Categories are a very crude and often misleading instrument. It is certainly worth observing that amongst occupations of the same class grouping some have higher rates of schizophrenics than others. For instance, dock labourers, newspaper sellers and watchmen, caretakers, and warehousemen contributed in one study (Carstairs *et al.*, 1955) fewer schizophrenics than their numbers warranted. On the other hand office cleaners, costers, hawkers, porters and kitchen hands contributed more than their fair share. In other words, it is important to observe intra-class as well as inter-class differences.

So far in this section we have considered evidence in connection with the 'drift' and 'drop' hypotheses, but, as was mentioned above, some authorities see the preponderance of schizophrenics in class V as the result of the conditions of life in the areas in which class V people live.

In 1939 Faris and Dunham found that the hospital admission rates for schizophrenia were higher in the central slum districts of Chicago than in the rest of the city. This, of course, does not imply that the patients themselves were poor or had always been so, but Faris later saw the disordered behaviour of the schizophrenic as an internalisation of what he took to be essentially disorganised slum areas. In connection with delinquency we have questioned whether slum areas are not disorganised, but organised on different principles to those of the observer, or whether some areas are not more disorganised than others. However, accepting for the moment Faris's view of disorganisation, it could be argued that the abnormal person drew on his essentially chaotic experience which he interpreted in his symptomatic behaviour. He internalised the confused norms of his culture, the contrasting groups to which he gave partial loyalty and the inconsistencies of promise and achievement in his own career. The disorganised social system in which he lived played a part in producing his marginal personality and also provided an environment inhospitable to him.

This question of the inhospitable environment is taken further by those who claim that formal social participation is associated with social class and that members of the lower classes lack access to sources which might provide help against personal malintegration. This isolation of the schizophrenic has received considerable emphasis in the sociological literature. It has been suggested that schizophrenia results from any form of isolation which cuts the person off from intimate social relations for an extended period of time. However, some schizophrenics become compulsorily sociable before their breakdown and gradually withdraw as the illness develops. The isolation in fact reflects unbearable conflicts, unbearable because self-involving. The schizophrenic rejects his self-image, but strives for social recognition. He is unable to communicate his conflict to others and may not have people accessible for communication. He then resorts to withdrawal as a medium of self-protection.

The sociological characterisation of mental illness

Sociologists often complain that their study of the kind of deviance called mental illness is hampered by the use of psychiatric categories which may be useful for doctors, but not for them. Some have tried to meet the need by attempting to categorise in sociological terms mental illness as a whole or particular illnesses. Lemert has suggested that mental illness should be seen sociologically as the disordering of the individual's symbolic process, meaning the emotive and cognitive processes which express and maintain an individual's attitudes towards his 'self'. The distortion in the symbolic process may take a number of forms, but all of them seem to be characterised by an extreme divergence between attitudes to self and attitudes of others. This divergence signifies the breakdown of social communication in such a way that the individual's self-concept does not reflect his society's definitions of himself. The mentally disordered person over-reacts or under-reacts to his 'self' and to 'others' in a larger number of situations than do other people. Thus, schizophrenics have been seen as persons in deep conflict over an intolerable loss of respect, to which there are three general ways of coping : drifting, the surrender to apathy, daydreaming (simple schizophrenia); delusional misrepresentation or fighting back (paranoid schizophrenia); panic (catatonic schizophrenia).

Cameron in relation to paranoid patients has developed the idea of the 'pseudo-community' or a network of subjective reactions created by a delusional process which peoples an imaginary social world. The high susceptibility of some people grows out of the unworkable attitude they have towards themselves as social objects; they have not been able to take the role of 'the other' and so view things more or less realistically; they either have no stable and dependable attitude or it is one of deprecation and condemnation. These individuals cannot share their social attitudes with 'others', to test them out. The individual is thrown back on himself to explain the slights etc. he receives. He organises his environment into a pseudo-community of attitude and intent. Gough (1948) has suggested that the psychopath is essentially a person who is deficient in role-playing, being unable to look upon himself as a social object or to play the role of 'the other'.

A critique of mental health concepts

It is possible, of course, to criticise the concepts of mental health from many points of view, logical, commonsensical, theological and so on. Concepts such as adjustment, psychological balance, wholeness etc. have become easy targets for a very wide variety of scepticism, partly because those who have used such terms in attempted definitions of mental health have been unaware of the rich potentialities for mirth to be found in the subject. Even in 1930 Wechsler was warning us that 'Enthusiastic mental hygiene tells us that it is concerned with the prevention of mental deficiency, criminality, the psychoneuroses, the psychoses, anti-social traits, family unhappiness, divorce, prostitution, alcoholism, sexual perversion, epilepsy and other such simple matters' (1930).

This seems bad enough but matters can be worse, as a perusal of Davis (1938) or Wootton (1959) will demonstrate. Davis, for instance, quotes the statement that 'Industrial unrest to a large degree means bad mental hygiene, and is to be corrected by good mental hygiene.' This is an ambiguous sentence, but even if industrial unrest was supposed only to lead to bad mental hygiene rather than being bad mental hygiene, there would seem to be no supporting evidence. Similarly, when the W.H.O. Expert Committee in 1951 added to a rather exhausting definition that mental health implies 'an individual whose personality has developed in a way which enables his potentially conflicting instinctive drives to find harmonious expression in the full realisation of his potentiality' (quoted by

Wootton, 1959), it is difficult to see what meaning can be attached to the words.

Sociologists have helped us to take this kind of criticism a stage further. Davis has argued, for example, that the ideas of the Mental Health Movement should be seen as an ideology, i.e. an interconnected set of ideas that are held with considerable conviction and can ultimately be seen as promoting the interests of particular groups. Davis analyses the definition of mental hygiene in terms of the following notions : (1) definitions are often *psychologistic*, in so far as social facts are explained in terms of the traits of individuals; (2) *individualistic*, since the emphasis is on individual happiness as the ultimate good, and on an individual's responsibility for his own destiny; (3) *rational*, since human welfare is judged to be attainable by the application of rational science. In addition, the Mental Health Movement acts on certain important social assumptions, including a mobile class structure, a competitive ethos and advancement as the goal of individual striving to which all else should be subordinated. These ideas and assumptions bear a striking resemblance to the Protestant open class ethic which first appeared as an ideology in the puritanism of the late sixteenth and early seventeenth centuries. This ideology emphasises the value of advancement by merit, worldly goods as the sign of spiritual prowess, sobriety and prudence in the attainment of goals, personal ambition, and a rationalistic utilitarianism.

This kind of sociological criticism is of considerable interest and use, but it needs to be refined. If the Mental Health Movement is an ideology we should investigate more closely its social origins and the groups in whose interests it might be developed and promulgated. We should also take seriously the more realistic attempts to find a more objective definition of mental health. This would constitute some kind of test of the argument that concepts of health, mental and physical, are essentially social in character (Lewis, 1953).

5
The family and social problems

The family as the 'basic' unit

'You know that the first government that ever was in this world was in a Family; and the first disorder that ever was in the world was in a Family; and all the disorders that ever fell out since sprung from Families. If Families had been better, Churches and Commonwealths all along had prospered. . . . Had young, and old, been right set before they entered into a Family : had the Family been founded in marriage in the Lord. Had relations betwixt wife and husband, children and parents, servants and masters been holily carried out according to the rule of Christ. Had the house been furnished with a wife . . . ; had it been furnished with a just getting and giving, it had been a thousand times better with Church, Commonwealth and Family, than it hath been, or is yet.'

This quotation from a seventeenth-century writer (Robert Abbott, *A Christian Family Builded by God*, 1653) typifies the importance that has been, and continues to be, placed on the family. It also illustrates the manner in which the family is seen as an institution carrying

74

major responsibility for and on behalf of 'the common-wealth', but not profoundly influenced and moved by social forces external to itself. The assumptions in this quotation, as in many other arguments, are that the family is 'the basic unit of society', that if all is well with families all will be well with society, and that 'bad' families create 'bad' commonwealths.

The first assumption, of the one-way traffic between the family and society, receives some encouragement from the relative isolation of the study of the family from the main stream of sociological work. Yet the family should be seen as mediating to family members the complex forces arising from social relations outside the family. It is for this reason that the family must have a central place in the study of social problems. The family contributes to the creation and the correction of problems because of its special relationship to other major social institutions and groups, not because 'pathological' families somehow produce all our social problems. The study of the family, then, for our present purposes must emphasise the interconnections between the family and the wider society. In this context the study of the role of the father assumes considerable importance, and it is strange that research workers have largely ignored this in their pursuit of 'the mother'. A recent study by McKinley (1964), though open to criticism on methodological grounds, is suggestive of the kind of insight that might be gained from a closer investigation of the role of father in the family and in the wider society. The father of a family places his family in society; it is his occupation that determines their position in the social world, that decides how much his family will obtain of the desired things (wealth, power, self-esteem and autonomy). Variation in class or status leads to variation in satisfaction and low status leads to two primary responses (aggression and compensating achievements in non-work areas of life) and to several secondary responses (e.g. regression, anxiety and submission). If the father fails in his achieved roles he is perhaps encouraged to place emphasis on his ascribed roles (e.g. his masculinity). This failure also rebounds throughout other areas of family life. Thus, McKinley suggests, the socialising techniques used by parents of the lower class are more severe and aggressively tinged than those used by parents of higher status. This reflects a response to the frustrations and aggressions experienced by the parents themselves in the class system. The father's deprived social position in the lower levels of society also results in a greater general hostility towards, and reduced involvement in, the emotional life of his adolescent sons.

The second assumption mentioned above, that 'bad' families produce all or a disproportionate share of our social problems, has certainly been operative in the work of social pathologists in this country in the present century. We saw in Chapter 1 that early in the century 'the social problem group' was seen as a pocket of pathological families responsible for a high proportion of a number of problems ranging from delinquency and alcoholism to rent arrears. More recently, it has been argued, without much supporting evidence, that so-called 'problem families' create a disproportionate number of social problems. This kind of approach to the study of social problems conceals the fact that these problems may have a close relationship to the values and structures which are regarded as socially normal. Goode (1961), for instance, quotes Crane Brinton to the effect that 'Bastardy and marriage in this world are quite complementary—you cannot have one without the other. In another world, you may indeed separate the two institutions and eliminate one of them, either by having marriage so perfect—in various senses—

that no one will ever commit fornication or adultery, or by having fornication so perfect that no one will ever "commit marriage". We cannot solve the problem of illegitimacy by simply deciding to define all children as legitimate. As long as no family unit has been established according to the norms of society the status of the child remains unchanged, and the role obligations of the "family" and the child's relatives will remain ambiguous. The radical changes necessary to eliminate illegitimacy almost completely would very likely come close to eliminating the family system, too.'

So far the argument has been concerned with correcting tendencies to see the family in isolation from the wider society and social problems as necessarily the products of family pathology. It is, however, important to recognise that family disturbance can make some contribution to the creation of social problems. The family mediates the forces and influences on the wider society, but it is not a kind of neutral conductor. The family does not simply provide the proscenium arch beneath which the class war, for example, is enacted; it 'makes a difference' to the way the forces and influences of the wider society are experienced within its boundaries. The study of social problems in the past has concentrated either on the contribution of family pathology or on the influence of such general factors as class or status. We need to take both sets of influence into account.

Part of the reason for this unbalanced approach to social problems lies in the rather uncritical way in which family pathology has been studied. Take, for instance, the concept of 'the broken home', which has been used as an explanation for many kinds of deviance. The concept suffers, of course, from considerable vagueness, and it is important to recognise that homes can be broken in different ways and for different reasons. A recent study showed that extra-marital conception was more common amongst certain groups of women from broken homes, particularly amongst women with separated or divorced parents and those brought up apart from their parents by unrelated persons or in institutions (Illsey and Thompson, 1961). We need, then, to concentrate more resources on the study of the family within its social context. We should, for example, attempt to classify and understand the various kinds of family disorganisation that can occur. Thus, Goode divides such disorganisation into: (a) the uncompleted family unit, the unmarried mother with her child; (b) family dissolution, annulment, separation, divorce, and 'job desertion'; (c) the 'empty shell' family; (d) the family crisis caused by 'external' events; (e) internal catastrophes which cause 'unwilled' major role failure through emotional, mental or physical pathologies (Goode, 1961). This kind of classification helps us to see that society is more concerned about some forms of disorganisation than others.

A way of looking at the family

Having established that a study of the family has relevance for the investigation of social problems, how can we describe the family in useful sociological terms? The crucial term appears to be that of role, and the important processes those of role-taking and role-making, on the one hand, and role-conflict and conflict-resolution, on the other. *Role* is a frequently used concept in sociology, and its use varies considerably. It can best be seen as a meaningful unit of behaviour deemed appropriate to the occupants of different kinds of social position (Turner, 1956). Sometimes this social position is formally defined, as in the case of the teacher, mother and so on. Sometimes the position is of a more informal nature (e.g. a leader, a 'Vicar of Bray type', and so on). At other times we wish to refer to someone who is 'placed' in society because he is identified with a particular social value. *Role*-taking refers to the imaginative playing of the role of the other in any series of transactions. In order to play an appropriate part in these transactions the persons concerned have to build up a picture of themselves as social objects, the objects of the others' perceptions and actions. This taking the role of 'the other' is an essential ingredient in *role-making*, which refers to the enactment of appropriate roles in any given situation. Role-making is not just a question of learning how to unpack all the 'oughts' from a box already labelled 'father' or 'son'; it is a more tentative and creative process. 'The actor is not the occupant of a position for which there is a neat set of rules . . . but a person who must act in the perspective supplied in part by his relationship to others whose actions reflect roles he must identify' (Turner, 1962).

Difficulties in playing roles—and the theatrical flavour is not entirely inappropriate, granted that we are thinking of acting according to such theorists and practitioners as Stanislavsky—arise from several sources. These can be divided into two main categories, those of inadequate resources and of conflict. The resources a person may lack for the appropriate playing of a role may be physical (as in the case of the head of a household who has no job) or intellectual and emotional (as in the case of the newly arrived immigrant). Conflicts can also be of different kinds. They may be due to a difference of definition and value between role partners. A wife comes to a marriage expecting, by and large, to play certain kinds of wifely role to a particular kind of role partner. Her expectations may be disappointed and met instead by her husband's conflicting expectations. Conflict can also arise between different role demands made on the same person.

A man may, for instance, be the focus of contrary expectations from the son-mother and the husband-wife relationships. Kerr (1958) has shown in her study of a group of slum families in Liverpool the ways in which a particular kind of introduction to role-playing brings families into conflict with the wider society. The personalities of the members of these families consist of simple role constellations: the roles are few and they tend to be rigidly defined and rigidly enacted. In the wider society, however, roles have become exceedingly complex, demanding greater powers of discrimination on the part of the individual who has to respond with appropriate action. These discriminatory powers develop with the increasing number of associations people make, and the increasing number of associations tend to link the person more firmly to the norms of his society. As Nadel (1957) has observed, 'the more roles an individual combines in his person, the more he is linked with persons in other roles and in diverse areas of social life. Equally, any additional role assumed by an individual ties him more firmly to the norms of his society.'

The central operations of the family are to be seen, then, as constituted by the processes of role-taking and role-making, role-conflict and conflict-resolution. These processes do not, of course, take place in a vacuum. They proceed and develop as a result of the operation of four main influences: the individual needs of family members, social norms, social goals and family identity. Each of these will now be separately considered.

Individual needs

Several attempts have been made to construct an exhaustive list of these needs. Murray, for example, uses the following terms to describe individual needs (1938):

dominance   (control of others)
deference   (admiration of, support of the actions of others)
autonomy   (freedom from restraint)
aggression   (opposition to, punishment of, another)
abasement   (surrender, self-belittlement)
achievement   (forceful exercise of abilities)
exhibition   (public exposition of the self)
play
affiliation   (friendly reciprocal relations)
rejection   (separation from and exclusion of others)
succorance   (gratification of needs through the actions of others)
nurturance   (gratification of needs of another through own actions)
infavoidance   (withdrawal from embarrassing situations)
defendance   (protection of self from the criticism of others)
counteraction   (striving for mastery in the face of failure)
understanding   (comprehending the relationships between ideas and experience)

Laing (1962) has a much shorter list which covers some of the same area as Murray. He sees individual needs as: the need to make a difference to another, to be recognised and to recognise oneself as a continuing entity by experiencing conformation of one's identity, and to be recognised as an agent. These examples demonstrate the important *social* behaviour that we describe in terms of 'individual needs', and one possible approach to the investigation of social problems would be to study the extent to which needs are differentially met in the different strata of society. Individual needs are clearly important, but it is difficult to be sure what they are in any detail, particularly at times of rapid social change. As Sprott has observed (1954), 'Every social system must satisfy certain basic needs of its members. The trouble here is that beyond such obvious needs as the provision of sufficient nourishment we hardly know what the basic needs are.' Nonetheless, in a sociological description of the family the category of individual needs is required even if we cannot always agree about its content. This perhaps requires emphasis at the present time when possible changes in social policy may be based on a rather monolithic view of 'the family as a whole'.

Social norms

It is easy to talk about norms, particularly if they are other people's. Indeed, the term is probably one of the most commonly used in sociology. Yet empirical investigation suggests that it is extremely difficult to discover either the norms which people say they observe or those that actually govern their behaviour. Bott, for instance, has suggested that even in a small-scale society norms are neither precise nor consistent. Consequently, in present western society it would be expected that the position was very much more complicated. In the small number of families studied by Bott (1957), 'informants found it very difficult to make familial norms explicit at all'. There were some points of agreement between couples but 'most of these were very vague and general and did not give a precise blueprint for action. On many points there was considerable variation from one couple to another.' The empirical study of norms, then, has not proceeded very far, but certain important general points can be made.

In the first place, reference is often made to 'the values' of a particular society, and it is sometimes easy to assume the existence of a value consensus in society instead of a possible hierarchy of values, with one or more exercising a dominant influence. We must, in other words, allow for differences between the values of different groups, as well as for conflict between them. A study of the norms upheld by a particular section of society concluded that the terms 'norm' and 'standard', though at present used interchangeably, should be reserved respectively for references to 'rules' observed by society at large (norms) and to 'rules' observed by particular groups (standards) (Baldamus and Timms, 1955).

Perhaps the most pertinent example of different standards upheld by different social groups can be found in social class differences in child-rearing. These have been quite extensively studied in America but some studies have begun to throw light on the British scene. Klein (1965) has recently contrasted the child-rearing practices of the deprived (the submerged 1/10), the traditional working class (both the 'roughs' and the 'respectables') and the middle class. In America a useful distinction has been made within the middle class between the bureaucratic family, with their emphasis on sociability, and the entrepreneurial, with the emphasis on ambition and independence. It is the latter group that attempt to inculcate in their children the ability to defer immediate gratification, which, argue Miller and Swanson (1958), is anachronistic in the contemporary welfare bureaucracy.

Secondly, it is important to consider the quality of the norms or standards that we wish to investigate. The terms 'norm' and 'standard' without qualification are only partially helpful. Merton (1957) has suggested six ways in which norms or standards might be differentiated.

Norms or standards may prescribe what ought to be done or proscribe what should be avoided. They may, alternatively, not be in this major key: they may instead indicate behaviour that is preferred or permitted. Norms may govern certain kinds of behaviour, but we also need to know whether there are not also recognised ways of circumventing the rules which are themselves institutionalised. Another kind of situation arises when two parties agree on the norms which should govern their behaviour, but may disagree on their actual application. Finally, norms may call for different kinds of conformity. This is of particular interest in view of the rather wholesale view sometimes taken of 'conformity'. Merton distinguishes between behavioural conformity (e.g. the Elizabethan ordinances in regard to the attendance of Catholics at Church of England services), attitudinal conformity (or a readiness to behave in a particular way when presented with certain cues), and doctrinal conformity, that is expressed verbally to others in public (as in Nazi Germany).

This kind of differentiation is of more than academic interest. Take, for example, the distinction betweeen prescriptive and proscriptive standards or norms. Members of certain religious groups are subject to the proscriptive standard, 'no alcoholic drink'. This means that there is no standard for the appropriate amounts of drink or the appropriate occasions for drinking. In this situation extremes of behaviour are likely if deviance occurs, since there is no guide and the drinking itself constitutes a rejection of previously accepted standards. Indeed these standards may help to produce extreme behaviour if they contain any reference to an anti-model, i.e. these standards could be reinforced by ideas of 'the dreadful example' of what happens to 'people who drink'. Mechanisms of this kind no doubt played a part in the creation of 'the fallen woman' in the past (Mizruchi, 1962).

Social goals

Here we are concerned with the social purposes of the family. These can be seen as the reproduction of legitimate children; status placement (which has obvious connections with family identity); biological maintenance (who gets help from whom and in what quantities); socialisation (how many members of which statuses are obliged to socialise and how long socialisation continues); the management of tension and the maintenance of behaviour patterns in the adults; and social control (Goode, 1961, b). Any one of these goals can be emphasised at the expense of others, and over-emphasis in one sphere is almost bound to lead to difficulty in another. For example, too much tension management of the adults will probably affect socialisation of the children. For reasons of space I cannot deal with all the social goals for which families strive, but we can take a brief look at the socialisation process since this is of basic importance. The most detailed and systematic account of this process is to be found in Parsons and Bales (1956, particularly Chapter II). This makes certain basic points. Firstly, socialisation (or the attempt to bring up children to be members of their particular society) is seen as a series of phases which proceed *discontinuously*, so that development consists of a series of crises, the successful resolution of each of which is necessary for the next stage; the results of each stage continue into the next.

Secondly, the crucial process for the organisation of the human personality as a system of action (and action can be defined as behaviour meaningful to the actor) is the internalisation of the successive series of social

85

systems into which the individual has come to be integrated in the course of his life. Parsons sees socialisation as the movement from the most simple social system (of mother-child identity) through a series of other systems (siblings and peers) to full adult status; this movement produces a series of internalised systems that correspond to the social reality.

At each stage, however, the child is not being socialised in the exclusive interests of that particular stage, and the parent or other socialising agent is doing more than play roles relevant to that particular stage. Thus, the mother-child identity should not exist independently as 'a society' but only in so far as the mother plays a role that represents the larger, more complex system, namely the family. We meet in family pathology, of course, cases of relatively closed mother-child societies. We can also see cases of fathers who feel unduly rejected by the necessary mother-child identity and feel unable to play their representative role of 'odd-person-*in*', someone, that is, who creates and maintains conditions for a satisfactory outcome of the mother-child society, sometimes by some unobtrusive referee work between the role-players. These 'representative' roles are of the greatest significance, since in any one phase of socialisation the socialising agent must play *two* main roles. He must be able to induct the 'other' into the role and then after a period lead him out. Parsons sees this process primarily in terms of what happens in therapy which, he claims, moves from permissiveness (limited participation with the 'deviant' on his own terms) through support and the denial of reciprocity to the manipulation of rewards.

Family identity

This is part and parcel of personal identity—I am one

of the Smiths who live in . . . I am one of a family that has a particular status in society, that wields power and influence and has power and influence wielded against it. This identity has, of course, its changing aspects, as the family goes through the various phases of its own natural history. There are a number of different ways of characterising these phases—Susser and Watson (1962), for example describe four phases :

expansion	beginning with the marriage and ending when the youngest child reaches adult status;
dispersion	beginning when the first child achieves adult status;
independence	beginning when all children are adult and have left home;
replacement	beginning when parents retire.

This family identity is closely linked with the important element of group cohesion or solidarity—the relative predominance of positive feeling between, and the moral respect amongst, the members. Cousins (1961) has recently outlined a number of factors in present-day society that threaten family solidarity. In the lower classes the importance of self-validation and self-advance runs counter to demands on the child that he should participate in a family solidarity. In society generally there are perhaps incompatibilities between the values exemplified in familial interaction and those expressed in other larger groups. The family may be seen as the main exponent of Christian virtues, but the peer group exemplifies rational self-interest. Parents can respond to splits between the family and other social groupings in a number of ways, as Cousins suggests. They can accept the situation and blame external events; they can continue their socialising efforts by effecting the child's withdrawal from situations that evoke deviant behaviour or—and this is of importance from the point of view of the contribution of the family to social problems—they can create a break, a discontinuity. For example, upper-class parents may tolerate a display of deviant behaviour provided it is restricted to interaction with peers—'that sort of talk is all right for your friends, but Mummy doesn't want to hear it.' Or a parent can continue to exact conformity, but he does so without an affective display of his own commitment—'you should behave in this way because this is the way to achieve goals that have been set for us by others.'

Family identity is also partly transmitted to us in terms of the groups we are told we resemble, the groups with which we should compare ourselves and those whose behaviour and standards we should follow. Such groups are usually described as reference groups, and they play a very important part in self- and family evaluation. As Mead (1934, p. 138) has remarked, 'The individual experiences himself as such, not directly, but only indirectly, from the particular standpoint of the individual members of the same group, or from the generalised standpoint of the social group as a whole to which he belongs.' It is also important to consider the groups to which an individual does not belong, but which constitute an important point of reference for him. This relationship is not, however, a simple one. It depends on whether or not he is eligible for group membership, and on his attitude towards the group (Merton, 1957). From this it follows that the process of changing reference groups is likely to be complex and hence stressful. Some of the complexity of this change has recently been demonstrated by Goldthorpe and Lockwood in their critical study of the often repeated proposition, 'We are all middle class now' (1963).

Conclusion

It has been suggested that the core operations in any family should be seen as revolving around role-making and -taking and role-conflict and resolution. These processes are influenced by individual needs, social standards and goals, social objectives and family identity. Each of these has been briefly discussed. In the course of this discussion incidental reference has been made to the way in which family pathology and social problems might arise. Thus, individual needs could be systematically frustrated or some gratified at the expense of others. Family members could be encouraged to adhere to deviant standards or to remain in a relatively closed mother-child society. Finally, changes in family identity brought about by a change in reference groups might create a situation of relative normlessness.

Generally speaking, however, there are perhaps two main ways in which the family contributes to social problems. In the first instance, the crucial processes may not occur. Thus, some families will not engage in role-conflict and hence in role-conflict resolution. In others, children will be unable to work through one particular phase of socialisation and will have to 'by-pass' the crises and solutions associated with it. Secondly, one of the processes can become closed, so that it does not interpenetrate the others and becomes in fact dominant. In this kind of situation standards can become closed against norms, socialisation against individual need, the acquisition of family identity against the attainment of social goals, and so on.

6

Summary and suggestions for further reading

Even the most cursory examination of the contemporary
or the historical scene suggests that social problems are
numerous. Such observations would find support in
Christian theology or in cynicism. Neither the doctrine
of original sin nor the conviction that we have some
choice only of the kind of difficulty we must endure
encourages any surprise at the existence of social problems. The sociologist goes beyond the common observation, the theologian and the cynic, and suggests that these
problems are 'natural', and that they proceed from certain
identifiable features of particular social structures. Durkheim argued, for instance, that crime was socially useful.
'But it serves only when reproved and repressed . . . It is
normal that there should be crimes, it is normal that
they should be punished' (1952, p. 362). More recently,
it has been claimed that 'societies create out of their
structure with predictable certainty the conditions of
social antagonism' (Dahrendorf, 1959). In this book it has
not been possible to study exhaustively all the social

problems that could be judged to be serious, either by the members of a society or by those attempting to analyse its structure. Nor have we been able to examine in detail all the sociological approaches that have been explored in the attempt to understand both social problems in general and particular problems, such as crime. The book has attempted to fulfil a number of more limited purposes, but in a way that is suggestive of wider themes.

In the first place, we have tried to discern the characteristics of a sociological approach. The motivation for this attempt was not a dogmatic purpose, but the desire to outline an area of potential usefulness. It was suggested that a sociological approach might revolve around the concepts of social relation and social structure. A sociological approach did not consist of a check-list of discreet characteristics (e.g. family income, educational attainment and so on), nor exclusively of factors that could be described as 'external'. The idea of the social relation emphasises the dynamic element of expectation, and suggests that sociological factors exercise their influence as much 'within' as 'outside' the individual. Such commonly used expressions as 'the social influences on behaviour' seem to imply that 'neutral' behaviour is from time to time pushed in one direction or another by external forces. Whereas these 'social influences' are a constituent feature of the behaviour.

Such an approach has advantages and difficulties when applied to the study of social problems. It suggests, first and foremost, that any aspect of social structure and any social relation might be relevant to the elucidation of any particular problem. In very simple terms, it must not be assumed that problematic features of a society are produced by other problematic features, that 'good' always leads to 'good'. Secondly, an emphasis on social structure encourages the exploration of the connections between social problems. Here we can see the influence of the conviction that 'social problems' are not only the problems acknowledged at any one time by the members of a particular society. Our society might, for instance, acknowledge the existence of a delinquency problem, a problem of unequal educational opportunity, of mental illness, and of poverty. Yet the idea of social structure leads us to question the value of conceptualising and investigating separate problems, and to ask instead more general questions, such as those concerning the existence of a fundamental *class* problem in our society. This is certainly a question worth asking, but sociologists are often too quick to answer it in terms of 'values' or other equally vague or ambiguous notions, or to suggest uplifting if unhelpful remedies. Thus, Mays (1963), in a work which attempts to view crime in the context of the social structure, states: 'I would myself advocate *the reconstitution of society*. I would like to see our social institutions overhauled and renovated to bring them into line with *agreed* moral purposes' (italics not original).

This quotation illustrates one of the more general difficulties of taking a sociological approach that emphasises social relation and social structure. As we saw in an earlier chapter, social relations are not directly observable: they can be deduced from a number of phenomena which, whilst observable in principle, are nonetheless very difficult to observe. These phenomena consisted of the actor's purpose, his expectation of the other's behaviour, the other's purposes and the actor's knowledge of them, the norms which the actor knows the other accepts, and, finally, the other's desire to win and keep the actor's approval. We saw in Chapter 5 that norms, for example, were in practice not easy to observe.

Before we can talk, then, in terms of social relation and social structure we need to invest in quite a considerable amount of preliminary work.

Preliminary work is also often required before we can be sure of the precise nature of the problems to be explained in terms of social relation and social structure. Thus, we have seen in connection with both delinquency and mental illness the necessity of preliminary work before we could discern the size and shape of the problem to be explored and explained. The mere existence of mental illness, delinquency and other social problems hardly arouses curiosity. What does require explanation, of course, are such facts as the much higher delinquency rates of boys compared to girls, the increase in delinquent acts and/or delinquents, the fact that some of us embark on delinquent careers and the majority still refrain from major delinquent acts.

Having outlined the main features of a sociological approach, we then turned to an illustration of some of the attempts sociologists had made to characterise social problems in general. The difficulties in a sociological approach mentioned above, and the difficulty of preventing concepts from sliding from a sociological to a psychological level, account for some of the differences in quality between the sociological works. A more important difference is to be found in theoretical orientation. In Chapter 2 an attempt was made to describe briefly approaches emphasising structure and those based more on a study of the process of deviation. In general sociological theorising a conflict and consensus model of society can be found, and both are judged necessary for a full understanding of society. Similarly, in the study of social problems we need an emphasis on forces arising from the interplay, either co-operative or conflictual, of different institutions and groups in the social structure, and also a recognition of the processes by which members of the society begin to follow and then maintain deviant careers.

The general approaches to social problems used by different sociologists should be studied and criticised as such, but it should be recognised that they should also illuminate the examination of particular social problems. From the many problems that could have been chosen it was decided to select delinquency and mental illness. This was partly because there seems to be general agreement that these conditions constitute important social problems, and partly because they have attracted considerable attention from sociologists and from other disciplines. Thus, in the case of delinquency it is instructive to compare the psychoanalytic approach which attempts a general explanation of delinquency in terms of the anti-social character with sociological explanations of more limited areas of the problem. Delinquency and mental illness are also fields in which we meet the difficulties of distinguishing the 'official' rate of the deviant condition from the 'real' rate, and we have seen that in the two fields both facets have to be considered if either is to be understood. We can, moreover, in these two fields see both the promise and the reality of a sociological approach. In delinquency we can recognise the important theory of the delinquent sub-culture, at the same time as we admit the paucity of attempts at empirical verification. In research in delinquency and mental illness we should acknowledge the comparatively small return in practical results that might lead to the improvement of means of dealing with these social problems. On the other hand, delinquency research has effectively questioned current myths about causation (Wootton, 1959), whilst the possible connection between social class and certain kinds of treatment for mental illness constitutes a very important area for further investigation.

So far we have outlined the argument that the study of social problems requires a consideration of social structure and social relations. It also requires the investigation of social processes whereby people become deviant. As Lemert has argued, a deviant person is one whose role, status, function and self-definition are shaped by how much deviation he engages in, by the degree of its social visibility, by the particular exposure he has to the social reaction to his deviant behaviour and by its nature and strength. Yet how do wider social forces impinge on the individual? It is here that we should consider the significance of the family.

The family has often been viewed as 'the cause' of many social problems. A favourite, if unsophisticated, explanation of juvenile delinquency, for example, is 'the parents'. This kind of explanation isolates one set of relationships within a family and tends to neglect the process of interaction even within that one relationship. We need, therefore, to be able to characterise the whole complex of relationships within a family. Hence the attempt in Chapter 5 to describe the core operations within a family, and to suggest that problems may arise when these operations are distorted or fail to take place. Thus, in certain families where role-conflict is not acknowledged a condition of pseudo-mutuality arises, leading possibly to schizophrenia in one member (Wynne *et al.*, 1960). We also need, however, to discern the ways in which the family is influenced by social factors 'outside' its boundaries, which it mediates to its members. Family relationships must be seen within the context of the wider society.

The study of the family has tended to be isolated from more general sociological theorising. The exploration of

95

social problems would profit from a more sustained investigation of the family, and this may well represent the most fruitful line of advance. If the family is studied within its social context and not as so many isolated self-contained nuclei, each producing its own specialised problem conditions, then this study should contribute not only to social problems but also to our understanding of society in general.

Guide to further reading

There are a number of general textbooks on social problems, all produced in America. The need for a text that would present a general theory of social problems applied to the problems experienced in Britain is striking. Amongst the several texts already published in America the following can be consulted with profit, provided the reader recognises the importance of discerning and bearing in mind the author's general approach along the lines indicated in Chapter 2.

Lemert, E. (1951) *Social Pathology*, New York: McGraw-Hill.

Elliott, M. and Merrill, F. (1961) *Social Disorganisation*, 4th edition, New York: Harper.

Dynes, R. *et al.* (1964) *Social Problems*, Oxford University Press.

LaPiere, R. (1954) *A Theory of Social Control*, New York: McGraw-Hill.

Merton, R. and Nisbet, R. (1961) *Contemporary Social Problems*, New York: Harcourt, Brace and World.

The two works that are most helpful as a general guide to clarifying the main approaches adopted by sociologists to the study of social problems are:

Dahrendorf, R. (1959) *Class and Class Conflict in Industrial Society*, London: Routledge and Kegan Paul.

Mills, C. Wright (1943) 'The Professional Ideology of the Social Pathologists', *American Journal of Sociology*, Vol. XLIX.

In general theorising about social problems the theory of 'anomie' has played a very conspicuous part. The main discussions of this theory are to be found in:

Merton, R. (1957) *Social Theory and Social Structure*, rev. ed. Glencoe: The Free Press; and in articles by Dubin, Cloward and Merton in the *American Sociological Review*, Vol. XXIV (1959).

Clinard, M. *et al.* (1964) *Anomie and Deviant Behaviour*, Glencoe: The Free Press.

Rose, G. (1966) 'Anomie and Deviant Behaviour—A Conceptual Framework for Empirical Studies', *British Journal of Sociology*, Vol. XVII, No. 1, March.

The last-named article appears to be the first general critical review of Merton's ideas to have been published in Britain.

Particular Social Problems

Books and articles in this section tend to fall into two main groups, those presenting the results of empirical research and those dealing with their subjects in a more general manner. Suggested reading on particular problems will be confined to the three main areas covered in the book.

Delinquency

A number of British books deal with the subject in a

general critical manner. Wootton, B. (1959) *Social Science and Social Pathology*, London: Allen and Unwin, examines the evidence for a number of hypotheses on the causation of crime. Mays, J. (1963) *Crime and the Social Structure*, London: Faber, attempts to link the study of crime to sociology, but his most enduring work will probably remain his first, rather impressionistic study (1954) *Growing Up in a City*, Liverpool University Press. The most thorough over-all treatment of the subject is the two-volume work, Mannheim, H. (1965) *Comparative Criminology*, London: Routledge and Kegan Paul.

The sub-cultural theory of crime has attracted a great deal of attention, and the most useful critical accounts are to be found in:

Downes, D. (1966) *The Delinquent Solution*, London: Routledge and Kegan Paul.

Matza, D. (1964) *Delinquency and Drift*, New York: Wiley.

A useful collection of articles and extracts from books has been edited by Wolfgang, M. (1962) *The Sociology of Crime and Delinquency*, London and New York: John Wiley and Sons.

Mental Illness

Useful material can be found in Susser, M. and Watson, W. (1962) *Sociology in Medicine*, Oxford University Press, and in Welford, A., ed., *Society* (1962).

On the connections between schizophrenia and social class the most interesting and recent work is Goldberg, E. and Morrison, S. (1963) 'Schizophrenia and Social Class', *British Journal of Psychiatry*, 109, pp. 785-802.

Goldberg, E. (1965) 'Working in the Community: What kind of help do People need?' *Social Work*, Vol. XXII, pp. 6-18, contains a good brief discussion of recent

research projects connected with the difficulties and possi-
bilities of the new programme of community care. Perhaps the quickest way to become acquainted with
American work on issues within 'therapeutic' organisations is to consult the collection of papers: Riessman, F.,
Cohen, J., and Pearl, A. (1964) eds., *Mental Health of the
Poor*, Glencoe: The Free Press.

Amongst a number of empirical projects mention should
be made of Kleiner, R. and Parker, S. 'Goal-striving, Social
Status, and Mental Disorder', *American Sociological Review*, 1963, Vol. XXVIII, pp. 189-203.

The Family

As was suggested in Chapter 5, a great deal of work
needs to be done on the connections between the family
and different social problems. There is no single work
that covers this topic, but useful ideas can be found in
the following works:

Goldberg, E. (1958) *Family Influences and Psycho-
somatic Illness*, London: Tavistock Publications.

Bell, N. and Vogel, E. (1960) eds. *A Modern Introduction
to the Family*, London: Routledge and Kegan Paul.

Kerr, M. (1958) *The People of Ship Street*, London:
Routledge and Kegan Paul.

Bibliography

ARGYLE, M. (1964) *Psychology and Social Problems*, London: Methuen.

BALDAMUS, W. and TIMMS, N. (1955) 'The Problem Family: A Sociological Approach', *British Journal of Sociology*, Vol. VI, pp. 318-327.

BERNSTEIN, B. (1964) 'Social Class, Speech Systems and Psychotherapy', in Riessman, F. *et al. Mental Health of the Poor*, Glencoe: The Free Press.

BORDUA, D. (1962) 'A Critique of Sociological Interpretation of Gang Delinquency', in Wolfgang, M. E. *et al. The Sociology of Crime and Delinquency*, London and New York: John Wiley.

BOTT, E. (1957) *Family and Social Network*, London: Tavistock Publications.

BROWN, G. and TOPPING, G. (1958) 'Post-hospital Adjustment of Chronic Mental Patients', *Lancet*, Vol. ii, pp. 685.

BROWN, G. *et al.* (1962) 'Influence of Family Life on the Course of Schizophrenic Illness', *British Journal of Preventive Social Medicine*, Vol. XVI, pp. 55-68.

CAMERON, N. (1956) 'The Paranoid Pseudo-Community' in *Mental Health and Mental Disorder*, ed. Rose, A., London: Routledge and Kegan Paul.

CARSTAIRS, G. M. *et al.* (1955) 'Changing Population of Mental Hospitals', *British Journal of Preventive Medicine*, Vol. IX, pp. 187-90.

CLAUSEN, J. and KAHN, H. (1959) 'Relation of schizophrenia to the social structure of a small city', in *Epidemiology of Mental Disorders*, ed. Pasamanick, B., Washington.

CLAUSEN, J. and YARROW, M. (1955) 'The Impact of Mental Illness on the Family', *Journal of Social Issues*, Vol. XI.

CLINARD, M. *et al.* (1964) *Anomie and Deviant Behaviour*, Glencoe: The Free Press.

CLOWARD, R. (1959) 'Illegitimate Means, Anomie and Deviant Behaviour', *American Sociological Review*, Vol. XXIV, pp. 164-76.

CLOWARD, R. and OHLIN, L. (1960) *Delinquency and Opportunity*, London: Routledge and Kegan Paul.

COHEN, A. (1955) *Delinquent Boys*, London: Routledge and Kegan Paul.

COHEN, A. and SHORT, H. (1958) 'Research in Delinquent Sub-cultures', *Journal of Social Issues*, Vol. XIV, pp. 20-37.

COHEN, Y. (1961) *Social Structure and Personality*, U.S.A.: Holt, Rinehart and Winston.

COUSINS, A. (1961) 'The Failure of Solidarity', in *A Modern Introduction to the Family*, ed. Bell, N. and Vogel, E., London: Routledge and Kegan Paul.

DAHRENDORF, R. (1959) *Class and Class Conflict in Industrial Society*, London: Routledge and Kegan Paul.

DAVIS, K. (1938) 'Mental Hygiene and the Class Structure', *Psychiatry*, Vol. I, pp. 55-65.

DOWNES, D. (1966) *The Delinquent Solution*, London: Routledge and Kegan Paul.

DUBIN, R. (1959) 'Deviant Behaviour and Social Structure: Continuities in Social Theory', *American Sociological Review*, Vol. XXIV, pp. 147-64.

DURKHEIM, E. (1894) *The Rules of Sociological Method*, Paris.

DURKHEIM, E. (1947) *The Division of Labour in Society*, Glencoe: The Free Press.

DURKHEIM, E. (1952) *Suicide: A Study in Sociology*, Eng. trans., London: Routledge and Kegan Paul.

DYNES, R. *et al.* (1964) *Social Problems*, Oxford University Press.

ELLIOTT, M. and MERRILL, F. (1961) *Social Disorganisation*, New York: Harper.

FARIS, R. and DUNHAM, H. (1960) *Mental Disorders in Urban Areas*, Chicago, Reprint of First Edition.

FIRTH, R. (1947) *Elements of Social Organisation*, Josiah Mason Lectures, Birmingham: Watts.

FREUD, S. (1935) *General Introduction to Psychoanalysis*, trans. J. Riviere, New York.

FRIEDLANDER, K. (1947) *The Psycho-analytical Approach to Juvenile Delinquency*, London: Routledge and Kegan Paul.

FULLER, R. (1939) 'The Problem of Teaching Social Problems', *American Journal of Sociology*, Vol. XLIV, pp. 415-25.

GILLIN, J. (1946) *Social Pathology*, New York and London: Appleton-Century.

GOFFMAN, I. (1961) *The Asylum*, New York: Doubleday.

GOLDBERG, E. and MORRISON, S. (1963) 'Schizophrenia and Social Class', *British Journal of Psychiatry*, 109, pp. 785-802.

GOLDTHORPE, J. and LOCKWOOD, D. (1963) 'Affluence and the British Class Structure', *Sociological Review*, Vol. XI, No. 2, pp. 153-63.

GOODE, W. (1961) (a) 'Family Disorganisation', in *Contemporary Social Problems*, ed. Merton and Nisbet, *op. cit.* 1961. (b) 'The Sociology of the Family', in *Sociology To-day*, ed. Merton *et al.*, U.S.A.: Basic Books.

GOUGH, H. (1948) 'A Sociological Theory of Psychopathy', *American Journal of Sociology*, Vol. LIII, pp. 359-66.

HOBSON, J. A. (1902) *The Social Problem: life and work*. London.

HOLLINGSHEAD, A. and REDLICH, F. (1958) *Social Class and Mental Illness*, New York: Wiley.

HYMAN, H. (1953) 'The Value Systems of Different Classes', in *Class, Status and Power*, ed. Bendix and Lipset, Glencoe: The Free Press.

HYMAN, H. and SKEATSLEY, P. (1954) 'The Authoritarian Personality—A Methodological Critique', in *Studies in the Scope and Method of the 'Authoritarian Personality'*, ed. Christie, R. and Jahoda, M., Glencoe: The Free Press.

ILLSEY, R. and THOMPSON, B. (1961) 'Women from Broken Homes', *Sociological Review*, Vol. IX, pp. 27–54.

KERR, M. (1958) *The People of Ship Street*, London: Routledge and Kegan Paul.

KESSEL, N. and SHEPHERD, M. (1962) 'Neurosis in Hospital and General Practice', *Journal of Mental Science*, 108, pp. 159-66.

KITSUSE, J. and DIETRICK, D. (1959) 'Delinquent Boys: A Critique', *American Sociological Review*, Vol. XXIV, pp. 208-15.

KLEIN, J. (1965) *Samples from English Cultures*, 2 vols., London: Routledge and Kegan Paul.

KOBRIN, S. (1951) 'The Conflict of Values in Delinquency Areas', *American Sociological Review*, Vol. XVI, pp. 653-61.

LAING, R. (1962) *The Self and Others*, Chicago: Quadrangle Books.

LANDER, B. and LANDER, N. (1964) 'Deprivation as a Cause of Delinquency: Economic or Moral', in *Mass Society*, ed. Rosenberg *et al.*, London: Macmillan.

LEACOCK, E. (1957) 'Three Social Variables and the Occurrence of Mental Disorder', in *Explorations in Social Psychiatry*, ed. Leighton, A. *et al.*, London: Tavistock Publications.

LEMERT, E. (1951) *Social Pathology*, New York: McGraw-Hill. (1964) 'Social Status, Social Control and Deviance', in Clinard, *op. cit.*

LEWIS, A. (1953) 'Health as a Social Concept', *British Journal of Sociology*, Vol. IV, pp. 109-24.

LITTLE, A. (1965) (a) 'The "Prevalence" of Recorded Delinquency, and Recidivism in England and Wales', *American Sociological Review*, Vol. XXX, pp. 260-63. (1965) (b) 'The Increase in Crime, 1952-62: An Empirical Analysis on Adolescent Offenders', *British Journal of Criminology*, Vol. V, pp. 77-82.

MAAS, H. (1955) 'Sociocultural Factors in Psychiatric Clinic Services for Children', *Smith College Studies in Social Work*, Vol. XXV, pp. 1-90.

MALZBERG, B., *Social and Biological Aspects of Disease*, quoted in Leacock, *op. cit.*

MATZA, D. and SYKES, G. (1961) 'Juvenile Delinquency and Subterranean Values', *American Sociological Review*, Vol. XXVII, pp. 712-19.

MAYS, J. (1963) *Crime and the Social Structure*, London: Faber.

MAYS, J. (1954) *Growing Up in a City*, Liverpool University Press.

MCKINLEY, D. (1964) *Social Class and Family Life*, Glencoe: The Free Press.

MEAD, G. (1934) *Mind, Self and Society*, University of Chicago Press.

Mental Deficiency (Wood) Committee, Report (1929) H.M.S.O.

MERTON, R. (1957) *Social Theory and Social Structure*, Glencoe: The Free Press. (1964) 'Anomie, Anomia and Social Interaction: Contexts of Deviant Behaviour', in Clinard, *op. cit.*

MERTON, R. and NISBET, R. (1961) *Contemporary Social Problems*, New York: Harcourt, Brace and World.

MILLER, D. and SWANSON, G. (1958) *The Changing American Parent*, New York: Wiley.

MILLER, S. M. (1964) 'The American Lower Classes: A Typological Approach', in Riessman, F. *et al.*, *Mental Health of the Poor*, Glencoe: The Free Press.

MILLER, S. M. and MISHLER, E. (1964) 'Social Class, Mental Illness, and American Psychiatry', in *Mental Health of the Poor*, ed. Riessman, F. *et al.*, Glencoe: The Free Press.

MILLER, W. B. (1958) 'Lower-Class Culture as a Generating Milieu of Gang Delinquency', *Journal of Social Issues*, Vol. XIV, pp. 5-19.

MILLS, C. WRIGHT (1943) 'The Professional Ideology of the Social Pathologists', *American Journal of Sociology*, Vol. XLIX, pp. 165-80.

MIZRUCHI, E. and PERRUCCI, R. (1962) 'Norm Qualities and Differential Effects of Deviant Behaviour: An Exploratory Analysis', *American Sociological Review*, Vol. XXVII, pp. 391-99.

MORRIS, T. (1957) *The Criminal Area*, London: Routledge and Kegan Paul.

MORRISON, S. (1959) 'Principles and Methods of Epidemiological Research and their application to Psychiatric Illness', *Journal of Mental Science*, 105, pp. 999-1011.

MURRAY, H. A. (1938) *Explorations in Personality*, Oxford University Press.

MYERS, J. and ROBERTS, B. (1959) *Family and Class Dynamics in Mental Illness*, New York: Wiley.

MYERS, J. and SCHAFFER, L. (1954) 'Social Stratification and Psychiatric Practice', *American Sociological Review*, Vol. XIX.

NADEL, S. F. (1957) *Theory of Social Structure*, London: Cohen and West.

ØEDOGAARD, O. (1936) 'Emigration and Mental Health', *Mental Hygiene*, Vol. XX, pp. 546-53.

PARK, R. (1952) *Human Communities: the city and human ecology*, Collected Papers, Glencoe: The Free Press.

PARK, R. *et al.* (1925) *The City*, University of Chicago Press.

PARSONS, T. and BALES, R. F. (1956) *Family, Socialization and Interaction Process*, London: Routledge and Kegan Paul.

POWER, M. (1962) 'Trends in Juvenile Delinquency', *The Times*, Aug. 9th.

RAPAPORT, R. (1960) *Community as Doctor*, London: Tavistock Publications.

REX, J. (1961) *Key Problems in Sociological Theory*, London: Routledge and Kegan Paul.

RIESSMAN, F. (1964) 'Are the Deprived Non-Verbal?' in *Mental Health of the Poor*, ed. Riessman, F. *et al.*, Glencoe: The Free Press.

ST. CLAIR DRAKE (1955) 'The Colour Problem in Britain', *Sociological Review*, iii, pp. 197-217.

SHAW, C. (1929) *Delinquency Areas*, University of Chicago Press.

SHAW, C. and MCKAY, H. (1942) *Juvenile Delinquency and Urban Areas*, Behaviour and Research Funds Monographs, Chicago.

SPINLEY, B. (1954) *The Deprived and the Privileged*, London: Routledge and Kegan Paul.

SPROTT, W. (1954) *Science and Social Action*, Josiah Mason Lectures, Birmingham: Watts.

SROLE, L. (1956) 'Social Integration and Certain Corollaries', *American Sociological Review*, Vol. XXI, pp. 709-16.

STANTON, A. and SCHWARZ, M. (1954) *The Mental Hospital*, New York: Basic Books.

STEIN, L. (1957) ' "Social Class" Gradient in Schizophrenia', *British Journal of Preventive Social Medicine*, Vol. XXI, pp. 181-95.

SUSSER, M. and WATSON, W. (1962) *Sociology in Medicine*, Oxford University Press.

SUTHERLAND, E. (1949) *White Collar Crime*, New York: Dryden Press.

SYKES, G. and MATZA, D. (1957) 'Techniques of Neutralisation', *American Sociological Review*, Vol. XXII, pp. 664-70.

THRASHER, F. (1936) *The Gang*, Chicago: University of Chicago Sociology Series.

TRASLER, G. (1962) *The Explanation of Criminality*, London: Routledge and Kegan Paul.

TURNER, R. (1956) 'Role-Taking, Role Standpoint, and Reference-Group Behaviour', *American Journal of Sociology*, Vol. LXI, pp. 316-28.

TURNER, R. (1962) 'Role-Taking: Process versus Conformity', in Rose, A. (ed.) *Human Behaviour and Social Processes*, London: Routledge and Kegan Paul.

WARDLE, C. (1962) 'Social Factors in the Major Functional Psychoses', in *Society*, ed. Welford, A.

WATTS, C. A. *et al.* (1964) 'Survey of Mental Illness in General Practice', *British Medical Journal*, ii, pp. 1351-59.

WEBB, B. and WEBB, S. (1932) *Methods of Social Study*, London: Longmans, Green.

WEBER, M. (1962) *Basic Concepts in Sociology*, London: Peter Owen.

WECHSLER, I. (1963) quoted in Ginsburg, S. *A Psychiatrist's Views on Social Issues*, Columbia University Press.

WEISS, R. and RIESSMAN, F., 'Social Problems and Disorganisation in the World of Work', in Merton and Nisbet, *op. cit.*

WILLETT, T. C. (1964) *Criminal on the Road*, London: Tavistock Publications.

WILSON, H. (1962) *Delinquency and Child Neglect*, London: Allen and Unwin.

WOOTTON, B. (1959) *Social Science and Social Pathology*, London: Allen and Unwin.

WYNNE, L., RYCKOFF, I., DAY, J. and HIRSCH, S. (1960) 'Pseudo-mutuality in the Family Relations of Schizophrenics', in Bell, N. and Vogel, E. (eds.) *A Modern Introduction to the Family*, London: Routledge and Kegan Paul.

YINGER, J. (1960) 'Contraculture and Sub-Culture', *American Sociological Review*, Vol. XXV, pp. 625-35.